Alastair
Sawday's

THE
Natural
Wedding
BOOK

Louise Moon

First edition
Published in the UK by
Alastair Sawday Publishing Co. Ltd in 2010

Alastair Sawday Publishing Co. Ltd
The Old Farmyard, Yanley Lane
Long Ashton
Bristol BS41 9LR
United Kingdom

This book was created by
Harris + Wilson ltd
18 Larkhall Place
Bath BA1 6SF
United Kingdom
www.harrisandwilson.co.uk

Text copyright © Louise Moon, www.ecomoon.co.uk
Image copyright © Marc Wilson (unless otherwise credited),
www.marcwilsonphotography.co.uk

Designed by 20 Twenty Design, www.20twentydesign.co.uk
Edited by Caroline Harris

ISBN-13: 978-1-906136-45-1

Alastair

Sawday's

THE
Natural
Wedding
BOOK

Louise Moon

Contents

16 The Style

36 The Venue

52 The Dress

74 Accessories

90 The Invites

106 The Menu

120 The Cake

138 The Flowers

154 Decorations

172 Natural Beauty

184 The Big Day

202   Wedding Planner

208   Directory

218   Seasonal Produce
        and Flowers

220   Index

224   Acknowledgements

Foreword by Jo Wood

You want your wedding day to be the best day of your life, so why not plan it with an organic, eco and ethical conscience, ensuring your values and personality shine through. From sourcing a unique, one-off vintage dress, to designing a locally sourced and seasonal menu, finding beautiful vintage crockery, or using a biodegradable marquee, there really is an eco choice out there for everyone.

The eco option can also be kinder on the purse strings, and offer you ways to make your day even more memorable, as I found when my daughter Leah got married in 2008. We used flowers from the garden, and collected jam jars to use as water glasses instead of hiring them. We even got a certificate from the council for all our recycling efforts.

If you don't have the time to research local suppliers and grow your own, then why not approach a sustainable catering company, to help get you started. I set up Mrs Paisley's Lashings, with leading eco chef Arthur Potts Dawson, with this in mind. A percentage of our profits go towards funding gardens in schools, so we can encourage the next generation towards healthy, organic eating.

I'm delighted that Louise Moon is sharing her expertise in green weddings; we all need to be making small steps towards a united global environmental change, and where better to begin than your wedding? Why not start married life as you mean to go on.

I wish you all the very best with planning your big day; love your planet, go organic.

Jo Wood, founder of Jo Wood Organics
London, 2010

Author's Introduction

My love of all things green and gorgeous started at an organic bed and breakfast in Dorset, many years ago. My fiancé and I ate delicious organic breakfasts, enjoyed their 100 per cent natural toiletries, browsed in the town's ethical shops, buying eco wares and the same natural shampoos and soaps, and left with changed priorities.

Not long after, I launched EcoMoon, my wedding planning business with a difference, designed to offer people a stylish alternative to the carbon-heavy and usually very expensive standard wedding. Current figures state that the average wedding can contribute 14.5 tonnes of carbon dioxide into the atmosphere – roughly double an individual human's carbon footprint for a year! This results in an expensive day, both for a couple's pockets and for the earth. So what is the alternative? Well, that is where my book comes in.

I wanted to write *The Natural Wedding Book* to provide couples with inspiration and advice on every aspect of their greener celebration, from vintage gowns to seasonal flowers, natural decorations to organic skincare, with gorgeous photographs to show their family and friends. As I have written it, I have included many hints and tips from my years of planning, as well as projects to make at home – everything from organic cupcakes to wedding day bags. It is my eco-chic guide to weddings for all couples, regardless of budget. No hairy shirts or mud in sight!

The Natural Wedding Book is here to dispel the myth that an eco-conscious wedding can't be stylish and look exactly like a 'regular' wedding, if that is what you wish for. Similarly, for couples wanting a unique, handmade day, then this is the book to show you how. With just a little effort and forethought your celebration can become a fabulous and individual event that will be a pleasure for you to plan.

So, now you have a copy of this book, I hope you enjoy using it and will carry it with you to dip into whenever you need a little advice or inspiration. At the end you will find a comprehensive directory of fabulous eco-friendly suppliers, artisan producers and generally good people.

Remember, whether dreaming of a formal celebration in a fairy-tale castle, or a festival-inspired event with tipis in the woods, planning a natural wedding should be enjoyable, stress free and about starting your married lives with dainty footprints on the earth.

Have a happy wedding!

Louise Moon, Bath, July 2010

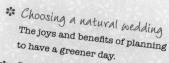

* **Choosing a natural wedding**
The joys and benefits of planning to have a greener day.

* **Seasonal wedding styles**
Choose your wedding style – from food to flowers, make the most of the time of year.

* **Vintage inspiration**
Go overboard with retro designs.

* **Eco-chic style**
Modern, minimalist and couture.

* **DIY and handmade**
Make your own wedding, with love and a wealth of creativity.

* **Getting practical**
Budgeting and choosing your ceremony.

* **Alternative stag and hen parties**
Plus greener ways to marry abroad.

The Style

You've just got engaged – congratulations! And now you're thinking about the kind of wedding you would like. Maybe you've considered being greener, or perhaps you're searching for ideas to help your budget go further, or to make your day truly special and unique. This chapter brings together themes and inspirations to engage your imagination, along with practicalities to help you on your way.

Deciding on a natural wedding

The beauty of deciding to have a naturally inspired wedding is the abundance of wonderful possibilities. For me, a natural wedding conjures up images of stunning, locally grown flowers and plants, flavoursome organic menus and artisan treats, gorgeous vintage bridal gowns and jewellery borrowed from a friend or relative, creative handmade invitations and relaxing, plant-based facials. And that is just the start.

Given half the chance, most couples would choose a green, natural and ethical day, but in my experience many simply do not know where to begin. You may already shop at your local farmer's market and take energy-saving measures at home, use natural cleaning and beauty products, or buy fairtrade whenever you can. But with so many choices to make when planning a wedding, along with the time pressures and the stress, it can often feel easier to go with the standard options.

The idea of this book is to give you some natural inspiration, and guide you through the information you'll need to make the choices that are best for you, and that are gentler on the environment.

Do just one thing...

I always say to couples planning their wedding, "If you can do just one thing…" and by this I mean one natural, eco-friendly or ethical thing. It could be choosing seasonal food, lighting the tables with plant-wax candles, or honeymooning at an eco boutique hotel. If every couple did this, it would make a real difference to the environmental effects of the wedding industry.

On average, a wedding puts 14.5 tonnes of carbon dioxide into the atmosphere – or twice your personal yearly carbon footprint. Food flown thousands of miles and travel by guests are the biggest factors. For peace of mind, consider the ethics and chemical content of some wedding products, too (see the Glossary on page 215).

Greener venues

Beaches, arboretums, village halls, charity-owned historic homes, parks, gardens, tipis and yurts.

Natural inspiration

Being eco-aware doesn't mean a wedding in scratchy dresses and muddy fields (although a field can be an amazing location). You could have a super-soft, hemp-silk couture gown made for your ceremony, then hold a barbecue on a sweeping crescent of beach. Or imagine brightly coloured, people-powered rickshaws, a woodland clearing as your setting, and favour boxes made from wildflower seed paper.

Choosing your wedding style

Spend time dipping in and choosing elements for your wedding style from the pages that follow. Whichever style you are drawn to, opt for organic and biodynamic food, grown according to eco-friendly guidelines, and fairtrade products that have been ethically made with the welfare of producers in mind (see the Directory on page 208).

Knowing that your wedding is having a positive effect on the environment is the perfect way for you to start your married lives. So be different, personalise your day and choose unusual venues, homemade food and a stunning ethical dress. You, your family and your guests will have an unforgettable day.

Wedding planner tip:
As you plan, take pleasure from meeting like-minded people and discover your creative side — and, most importantly, have fun.

Seasonal weddings

From springtime tulips to brink-of-autumn echinaceas, make the most of seasonal flowers and foliage, and enjoy foods at the peak of their flavour. Fruit, vegetables and flowers that can be grown naturally outdoors in your region reduce the need for preservatives or artificial climates. Local produce has less distance to travel, so helping to cut your wedding's carbon footprint.

Let the time of the year when you are marrying inspire your choice of wedding location and dress. Marquees, tipis and yurts are perfect for the summer while eco-chic hotels, historic homes and modern green wedding venues suit cooler winter weather. Often, the surrounding landscape will present the best backdrops to your photographs. Link hands beneath blossoming trees for a natural confetti shot.

Food through the year

Hot comfort food, with rich sauces and deep flavours, will warm up winter-themed weddings. Light, fresh tastes, from tingling fruit sorbets to many-coloured salads, are ideal for celebrations in the summer. Organically grown fruit and flowers avoid the synthetic pesticides that are common elsewhere in agriculture. If you find organic produce too expensive to buy, try growing your own (see page 112). Or discover food for free, by foraging the likes of star-flowered wild garlic on a long country walk.

Making the seasons your wedding style

Any couple can have a celebration that is sensitive to the seasons, whether you already lead an eco-friendly lifestyle or not. Personalise your day with seasonal elements chosen for the time of year: natural fabrics, such as cool linen or gentle wool knits, skincare treats with local strawberries (see page 180), or a bouquet of cornflowers you have tied yourself (see page 146). For timely themes, think of country garden, autumn colours, summer sun, winter chill, spring blossom, village fête.

All about flowers

Try making flowers the focus of your wedding design – or even a single flower variety. It's a simple way to create an effortlessly coordinated look.

❀ Commission an artist to draw your chosen flower and use the illustration for invitations, menus and orders of service.

❀ Use the same flowers for table decorations and bouquets.

❀ Break apart flower heads to make fresh petal confetti (see page 152).

❀ Ice a floral design on to homemade biscuits for your favours.

❀ Decorate your cake with fresh flowerbuds.

❀ Wear a single bloom in your hair.

Rich pickings

❀ Pick-your-own strawberries, blueberries and raspberries.

❀ Brightly coloured squashes.

❀ Winter root vegetables.

❀ Homemade elderflower cordial.

❀ Cider made from local scrumpy apples.

❀ Locally caught fish or free-range local meat in its prime season.

❀ Homemade seasonal jams.

❀ Home-baked cakes decorated with seasonal fruit or flowers.

❀ Wildflowers grown in your garden.

❀ Berries and seedheads for your decorations.

Natural advantages

Locally grown, seasonal food and flowers mean fewer food miles, and support local farmers and enterprises.

Vintage weddings

Indulge your vintage side and bring together all those little gems collected over the years: the beaded Italian bag, the fabulous 1950s wedding gown, the Edwardian pearl necklace and the long, elegant gloves. Antique, second-hand and re-used items are great for the environment. They are effectively carbon neutral as they have already been used, and you may well be saving them from being thrown away.

Charity shops are a fantastic source of unexpected finds – buying from them will benefit both the good cause and your wallet. Relatives may also have heirloom jewellery, ceramics or linen to pass down to you. Don't be afraid to use items that do not match – it can create a delightfully eclectic look.

Stylish couples

Take inspiration from these classic 20th-century weddings.

* **Grace Kelly and Prince Rainier**

    A fairy-tale wedding in Monaco in 1956, in front of the world's press and the adoring public. She wore a full-skirted gown, crafted from ivory silk taffeta and lace.

* **Edward and Mrs Simpson**

    They married in 1937 in France, shortly after he renounced the British throne. She wore an elegant, cream, long-sleeved skirt suit, complete with neat, covered-button detailing and stylish hat, and carried a small matching bag.

* **Yoko Ono and John Lennon**

    1960s fashion at its best. They married in Gibraltar in 1969; Yoko wore a white crêpe mini dress, white knee-socks and a wide-brimmed hat.

Setting up your own garden party

Marry in a local church, then walk to your reception in a friend's flower-filled garden. Decorate a traditional marquee with homemade bunting and vintage vases filled with cottage-garden flowers. An elegant string quartet, or friends busking, is the perfect accompaniment. As the sun goes down, light soya candles in recycled jam jams.

* Hired furniture should arrive the night before, and be stored under cover.

* Make sure there is enough room for people to walk between back-to-back chairs.

* Layering vintage tablecloths will disguise ordinary tables, or spread lengths of vintage sari fabric over plain white cloths.

* Arrange flowers the night before, then keep them somewhere cool and dark.

Style from the past

* Eclectic floral china.
* Retro 1960s coloured glass vases.
* Antique suitcases.
* Beautiful lace dresses.
* Original printing stamps.
* Chic vanity cases.
* Vintage *Vogue* magazines.
* Heavy linen tablecloths.
* Heirloom veils.
* Long white gloves.
* Inherited jewellery.
* Salvaged dress patterns.

Natural advantages

Retro gowns, country-style tea parties, florals and polkadots – re-using is effectively carbon neutral and reduces what might otherwise go to waste.

Eco-chic weddings

From urban eco boutique hotels to innovative organic catering, you can have a big day that is contemporary, chic and green, too. There's no need to compromise your taste. Revel in the growing range of eco designer labels and bespoke makers, such as Jessica Charleston, who created the kimono-inspired dress opposite (see the Directory on page 208). If you have a smaller budget, there are ways to create a sleek, modern look for less – take a look at the list on the left.

Eco stores and suppliers can provide you with wedding products designed specifically to minimise your carbon impact. Most of these also have outstanding ethics. You can find everything from designer organic cakes to beautiful recycled paper stationery and artisan wooden place names.

Simplicity itself

Fill straight-sided, contemporary glass bowls with organic white roses for minimalist floral displays, choose modern ethical fabrics such as hemp silk (see page 64), decorate tables with driftwood and have a clean-lined, white-iced artisan-made cake, decorated with artfully placed fresh flowers and pale green recycled ribbon.

* High-tech organic skincare – luxurious natural brands and make-up free from synthetic chemicals (see page 175).
* City-centre eco hotels – minimalist and low-impact.
* Biodynamic wines – some of the world's top vineyards use this approach.
* Peace silk – a light, ethical fabric for a handmade gown.
* Fairtrade artisan chocolate – for favours and cakes.
* Limited editions – support local artists by choosing handmade decorations.
* Contemporary ethical jewellery – from certified diamonds to local hardwood rings (see page 79).
* Recycled glass – and jewellery made from luminous sea-glass beads, shaped by the ocean (see opposite and page 80).
* Designer organic cakes – visually stunning, in any shape you can imagine.
* Bespoke bouquets – use fairtrade flowers to complement your dress, or grow your own sculptural flowers and foliage (see page 143).
* Hired topiary – add elegance with formal box balls or a cloud-pruned olive.
* Eco gift lists – from stylish green designer names.
* Biofuel wedding cars – or go low-tech with bicycles.

Modern for less

* Beachcombed pebbles as name tags.
* Single flower stems in recycled bottles.
* Paperless designer e-vites (www.paperlesspost.com)
* Natural soaps for favours.
* A simple, chic colour scheme, such as stylish black and white.
* White linen tablecloths.
* A simple dress with contemporary eco jewellery.
* Barbecue on the beach.
* White-iced cupcakes on a hired, tiered stand.
* Sky lanterns.
* Cool camping for your honeymoon.

Natural advantages

Green designer services often focus on energy-saving and re-using and recycling, and have strong ethical policies.

Handmade weddings

A DIY wedding can be enormous fun to create. Homemade cakes, decorations, invites and dresses can really personalise your day, while also saving you money. Relax in the knowledge that your wedding will be distinctive and perfectly you.

To ensure your DIY wedding is memorably stylish, coordinate your stationery, match flowers to dress details, and choose decorations that complement your venue.

Picture the scene: trees looped with homemade gingham bunting, tables laid with plates of family food and grandma's chutney. Pretty name cards, showing guests their seats, crafted out of recycled paper and reclaimed lace. A wedding gown made by the bride from a vintage pattern. Flowers and herbs planted into coir pots and small enamel jugs by a friend, and grouped as table displays. Perfect.

Family and friends

Depending on the size of your wedding, you may need an extra pair of hands to craft your day. Ask relatives to help out and make the cake, or a plate of food. Or gather bridesmaids together for an evening of jewellery-making. Invite a talented friend to take the photographs, and see if older family members have gowns squirreled away that can be reworked into something wonderful.

Get your groom involved and persuade him to make the chocolate truffle favours – easy to prepare, and delicious. Pack into biodegradable cellophane bags and tie with natural raffia for wedding-day gifts. Spend time with friends creating your own recycled fabric corsages, and embellish a guest book using the same materials.

Handmade and bespoke

If hand-crafting isn't for you, or you are not confident of your skills, search out talented local artisans who can make everything from your dress to the bread.

Homemade tips

* Borrow books from the library to find out how to make invitations (see page 98).
* Find local courses in traditional printing techniques and jewellery-making.
* Salvage charming old fabrics to make corsages, bunting and tablecloths.
* 'Ladies-a-plate' is a New Zealand tradition where female guests bring a dish of homemade food – or ask all the cooks among your guests, male and female.
* Bake your own cupcakes and decorate imaginatively (see page 126).
* Find a local dressmaker and have a gown made to measure, or ask a friend or relative to make it for you (see page 62).
* Gather flowers from your garden and tie your own bouquet.
* Make timber signs for the reception with your groom.

Your DIY wedding preparation kit

* Salvaged fabrics.
* Recycled old ribbons and lace.
* Antique printing kits.
* Pebbles and beads.
* Natural raffia.
* Pinking shears and sharp scissors.
* Handmade paper.
* A sewing kit and sewing machine.
* Plenty of time – and, of course, this book.

Natural advantages

Lovingly handmade food, dresses and decorations can reduce packaging and food miles, and DIY is an excellent thrifty choice.

Pawle and
Kiki,
love, laughter,
and happy times
4 ever ♡
lov,
Rachel + Martin
xx

Budgets and priorities

The budget can be a major influence on your day. But regardless of whether you have been saving for years or are strapped for cash, you can still have a glorious wedding. Don't be tempted to borrow money for your celebration – in my experience this simply leads to stress and worry. It is better to start your married lives together without this burden.

My advice to all couples at the beginning of the planning phase is to make a list of your wedding priorities. You may have your eye on a special designer dress, or be desperate to invite 200 guests, so working out what matters most to you is a good starting point.

Wedding planner tip:
Add up your spending as you go along so you don't go over budget. Simple advice, but surprisingly effective.

Once you have your list, allocate sums of money that you are prepared to spend. Some wedding books and magazines suggest percentages for each wedding item, from the dress to the music. But if you follow these you may end up spending more than you want on some things. Instead, simply divide up your budget according to your own priorities.

Being inventive

A natural wedding allows you to be resourceful and creative with your spending. If you decide to blow most of the budget on food, see if you can borrow a dress, or if you simply cannot afford stationery, send out e-vites instead.

Don't be afraid to ask friends and relatives for their help and advice. They will often be happy to make food, provide bunches of flowers from their gardens, or lend pieces of jewellery or even a wedding dress. Make the most of their skills: ask if they can style your hair, apply your make-up, or even teach you how to lino-cut your own invitations. They will almost certainly love to be involved.

Natural choices

You will probably have ideas about one aspect of your wedding where it really matters to you to be as green and ethical as possible. Whether it is organic food, vintage collectables, eco-friendly products or the perfect green venue, put this in your wedding priority list and remember to bear it in mind when searching out suppliers.

It is easy to lose direction when planning a wedding, panic-buying things that you don't need and won't use. By re-reading your list and thinking about whether you really need a product, you can stick to your ethical principles and keep a rein on your budget.

For more planning help, see our Natural Wedding Planner on page 202.

Your ceremony

The ceremony is the keystone of your wedding and will define your day. There are many different ways to wed, whether you dream of a traditional church service or an alternative ritual, prefer a civil route or decide to 'marry' without any official, legal ceremony. Rules and regulations differ in every country, so check with your local authority on what constitutes a legal marriage in your area. There are meaningful ceremonies for couples of all faiths; this quick guide will get you started.

Legalities

The requirements for a legal marriage vary from country to country and can be confusing. In the UK, you can be legally married in a church or other religious building, in a council registry office or at a registered venue by a registrar. Outdoor marriages are more difficult and are only currently legal for humanists in Scotland. To marry legally outdoors in England, Ireland and Wales the ceremony must take place under a registered shelter, usually in the grounds of a stately home or hotel.

Humanist weddings

In Scotland, Australia, New Zealand, Canada, Norway and some states in the USA, humanist weddings are legal. These are non-religious weddings where couples are encouraged to write their own vows and choose their own music and readings. Ceremonies must be conducted by a registered celebrant but can take place at any location as long as it is 'safe and dignified'. Whether under a blossoming tree or on a deserted beach, the possibilities for a humanist wedding are truly special.

Gay and lesbian weddings

The laws vary across the globe. In the UK, civil partnerships (for gay and lesbian couples) are legal in council registry offices and some registered venues. Other countries, such as the USA, allow civil partnerships in certain states, while some do not allow same-sex weddings at all. Any couple can choose to have a non-legal commitment ceremony – you could even have a friend conduct the wedding.

Hand-fastings

A hand-fasting is an ancient pagan ceremony popular in many countries. During the ceremony, the couple's hands are tied together with a piece of ribbon, fabric or cord. When tied tightly in a knot, this signifies that the couple's union is permanent. This is where the saying 'tying the knot' originates. Hand-fastings are usually held in woodland with guests stood in a circle marked with stones. They are beautiful ceremonies and can be combined with a civil wedding for a legal marriage.

It's your day

Unless you are having a formal religious service, generally you can have some input into the design of the ceremony. Personalise your day by writing your own wedding vows, and choosing readings, poetry and music that are special to you both.

Eco photography

It's simple to be green with your photos – just go digital. Ask your photographer to provide the images on a CD so you can view and print them as you wish. Traditional photo-printing techniques use synthetic chemicals, so instead print on to recycled paper using vegetable-based inks – see the Directory for specialist printers.

Wedding albums often have tropical hardwood covers that are sourced from Australia and New Zealand. If you live in the UK, the carbon footprint of the album alone is huge. Choose a company that provides locally produced, handmade paper albums with sustainably sourced timber covers. Old-fashioned, self-adhesive photo-corners are preferable to spray glue.

Your wedding notebook – save cuttings, business cards, fabrics and pictures showing ideas you like into a book to help you design your day.

Tattered & Torn

A DATE TO REMEMBER

Celastrina argiolus

7 ♥

♠7 Holly Blue
23-30mm ♠7

...ath Organic Blooms at ...he Walled Garden

Bath Organic Blooms

Further afield and pre-celebrations

If you plan to marry abroad, with a little thought, it is still possible to have an eco-friendly wedding. A diverse and growing range of eco hotels and lodges across the world use organic food and local suppliers, have recycling strategies and green electricity tariffs, and promote fairtrade. For peace of mind, ask the same questions you would of a venue closer to home – see page 38.

Think about how you intend to get there – travelling by train is better for the environment than flying – and consider offsetting your journey through accredited schemes such as www.carbonfootprint.com.

The legalities of marrying abroad vary from country to country. Most will require you to be 'resident' for anything from a couple of days to a few weeks. Be prepared to provide a bundle of paperwork, including passports

and birth certificates, and sometimes a letter from your consulate. Unless you both speak the local language an interpreter is essential. Check with the country's consulate for specific requirements and advice.

Alternative stag and hen parties

Stag parties and hen dos are a long-standing wedding tradition. But why not try something a little different? Friends of mine held a joint hen and stag mini festival in a friend's field. They erected a marquee and invited local bands and DJs to play. Guests camped for the whole weekend and brought food to share.

Cheap flights to typical party destinations create large carbon footprints, so stay closer to home and take public transport or car-share. See the box above for more ideas.

Dare-to-be-different stags

❋ Outward bound weekends.

❋ Survival courses.

❋ Mountaineering trips.

❋ Hiking breaks.

Fashionably individual hens

❋ Crafting weekends.

❋ Spa breaks.

❋ Glamping – 'glamorous camping'.

❋ Home cocktail parties, complete with a professional mixologist.

Packing for a bride abroad

Transporting a wedding dress can be a challenge – follow these tips for stress-free packing.

❋ Choose a dress in a fabric that will not crease easily – such as silk.

❋ A shorter dress or skirt suit is much easier to transport than a long gown.

❋ Place layers of acid-free tissue paper between the folds of your gown to minimise creasing.

❋ Vintage dresses often travel more happily than you would expect, as the beading and lace can disguise wrinkles.

❋ Small, beaded vintage purses make a stylish alternative to a bouquet and take up minimal space.

Wedding planner tip:
Expensive hen and stag celebrations can be too costly for some friends. More affordable activities will make it easier for them to join in.

* **What makes a venue green**
  The essential questions to ask.

* **Eco-chic wedding locations**
  From boutique hotels to organic
  bed and breakfast.

* **Weddings under canvas**
  Yurts, tipis and traditional Cruck marquees.

* **Heritage and historic buildings**
  From romantic castles to working mills.

* **The great outdoors**
  Beaches, arboretums and wildlife centres.

* **Going local**
  Neighbourhood halls, friends' gardens and
  top tips on hiring.

* **Easy and stylish transformations**
  Including a beautiful chair decoration.

The Venue

Choosing your wedding venue will be one of your
first and biggest decisions, so you'll want it to reflect
your values as a couple. There are plenty of charity,
thrifty and naturally luxurious alternatives to the
standard hotel wedding package (even though some
chains are trying to be more eco-friendly). You can
hold your reception, and sometimes marry, anywhere
from a yurt in a friend's garden, to an eco-chic
boutique hotel, or a sumptuous historic house.

What makes a venue green

There is a stylish green venue for every celebration, whatever your beliefs or religion. The best way to find a venue is by personal recommendation, but guides and websites can also help. Alastair Sawday's *Venues in Britain* (www.sawdays.co.uk) uses a questionnaire to determine the efforts that venues are making to be ethical and environmentally friendly, while www.greenunion.co.uk, www.ecofriendlyweddings.co.uk and www.ecohotelsoftheworld.com also vet their entries.

The questions on the notepaper below will help you to establish a venue's environmental credentials. You may have your eye on a fantastic place that doesn't fulfil all of these criteria, but some effort is better than none. It is up to you to decide what matters most to you.

Questions to ask a venue

❋ Does it have a recycling and waste management strategy?

❋ Does its energy come from a green energy provider, or does the venue generate its own through on-site renewables such as solar panels?

❋ Do the managers use local suppliers where possible?

❋ Do they choose fairtrade products?

❋ Do they opt for organic food, and is it grown on site or locally?

❋ Do they clean using products that are free from petroleum-based and synthetic chemicals?

Energy use

Many buildings, from farms to modern hotels, now generate their own electricity. Greener venues may have a biomass boiler or a wind turbine, solar thermal panels or photovoltaics. Or they should at least buy their energy from a green provider.

Waste strategy

These days there is little excuse not to recycle, and food waste is easily composted. However, some venues will go further in reducing, re-using and recycling. Winkworth Farm in Wiltshire bottles its own water and re-uses the glass bottles.

Reducing chemical exposure

Many people are now aware of chemicals such as volatile organic compounds (VOCs) that can affect health. Look for venues that decorate using natural paints and water-based varnishes, use gentle, non-synthetic cleaning products, and have chosen furnishings that are made using natural materials or meet strict eco standards, such as the Nordic Swan eco-label.

Organic food and products

As well as cooking you a delicious organic wedding breakfast, venues can offer many other options, such as organic cotton bedding (regular cotton uses a quarter of the world's pesticides), organic bamboo towels, organic plant-wax candles and organic toiletries. For more about organics and certification, see page 110.

Air-conditioning

Air-handling units (AHUs) use massive amounts of energy and also cause noise pollution. Even in hot and humid conditions well-designed venues can cool their buildings naturally though windows and roof vents, but if there is air-conditioning, check it is powered by renewable energy.

This is a giant hat kata style of tipi, which can be joined in combinations to make different-sized spaces, from www.papakata.co.uk.

Before you start your venue search, it is useful to determine some basic principles:

❋ Would you like to marry and hold the reception in the same location?

❋ Do you need a venue licensed for marriages? (Not required for hand-fastings or blessings.)

❋ How many guests do you plan to invite?

❋ Do you want the ceremony or reception to be inside or outdoors?

❋ What time of year do you wish to marry?

Consider how your venue fits with your vision. If you are planning a formal affair with floor-length gowns and a lavish sit-down meal, a grand historic venue would be ideal. With an eco-fabric dress, flowers in your hair and a barbecue, a tipi in a field may be just right.

For more about the legalities and licensing, see page 30. If you are marrying abroad, see page 35.

Wedding venue ideas

❋ 10 guests – small timber-framed Cruck marquee in a friend's flower-filled garden, near a tiny, local church.

❋ 50 guests – civil ceremony and sit-down dinner at an eco boutique hotel.

❋ 100 guests – civil ceremony at a licensed, organic eco centre with outdoor drinks reception.

❋ 200 guests – festival-inspired hand-fasting under a tree, followed by a reception in a giant tipi.

Wedding planner tip:
To minimise guest miles and keep your wedding carbon footprint low, hold your ceremony and reception at the same venue.

From top: Penrhos Court, views at Winkworth Farm, Dauntsey's School, The Pump Room in Bath, Forever Green eco centre.

Eco hotels and centres

Specialist green wedding venues can range from purpose-built eco centres, constructed using locally sourced materials and sustainable building techniques, to carefully renovated buildings upgraded to the highest environmental standards. Often they will also grow their own food and flowers.

Eco venues usually advertise their credentials, but if there is something specific that you are concerned about, do ask – they are generally happy to help. The Directory on page 208 lists some of our favourites.

Many hotels and eco centres are licensed for civil ceremonies, while others may have chapels in their grounds, and some are set up to host the perfect hand-fasting (see page 30). Check which type of ceremony they can perform before you book the date.

Eco boutique hotels

Often elegant town house conversions or innovative new builds with holistic spas and contemporary interior design, these score highly on the eco credentials but do not compromise on luxury or comfort. The Scarlet in Cornwall (www.scarlethotel.co.uk), for example, has a biomass boiler and natural ventilation system, plus a solar-heated swimming pool and a restaurant run by a Michelin-starred chef. Find other eco hotels around the world at Organic Places to Stay (www.organicholidays.co.uk).

Organic hotels and bed and breakfast

These tend to be smaller and more low-key than eco boutique hotels. They aim to be as green, ethical and sustainable as possible, and use organic products from soft, unbleached cotton sheets to organic shower gel. Ideal for more intimate weddings, some organic hotels have their own wildflower gardens or private beaches. Moss Grove Organic (www.mossgrove.com) in the Lake District was refurbished using clay paints, wool insulation and reclaimed stained glass.

Sheepdrove Organic Farm
Berkshire, United Kingdom

Architect designed, with rammed-earth walls and a timber frame, Sheepdrove (www.sheepdrove.com) is a fine example of an eco centre. The contemporary interior finishes include natural paints and recycled doors. Licensed for civil ceremonies, all the food is organic and local, much of it grown on the 2,300-acre organic working farm – they even grow wheat for artisan bread.

Specialist green wedding venues

Specifically designed or renovated to provide the ideal setting for a natural wedding, venues such as Sheepdrove (above) have the highest environmental standards. Some are entirely wind or solar powered. Most will provide all you need for your day, from locally grown flowers to organic food and their own free-range eggs. Look out for those that offer something different for your guests, such as a garden maze, a seawater swimming pool, or a stone circle. Many are surrounded by beautiful, organic gardens – a wonderful setting for an idyllic wedding.

Wedding planner tip:
Think about how far your guests will need to travel to your wedding. Long journeys have large carbon footprints.

Weddings under canvas

Holding a reception under canvas is an exciting prospect and a practical solution for couples with a large guest list but not the budget to match. Marquees, tipis, yurts and Bedouin tents offer fantastic opportunities for unusual and striking decorations, and an outdoor reception gives a relaxed, informal feeling to the day.

Fields and farms can provide the perfect setting. Often farmers will rent out a field for a day or weekend; some will even provide local produce. Ask if you can borrow straw bales for seating, and whether there are toilets nearby for your guests. Always check with the relevant authorities if you need either a marquee or liquor licence for the event, and make sure there is access for your tent hire company and any guests with disabilities. You can set up a small kitchen tent and hire catering equipment, although food prepared beforehand will mean less fuss. See page 116 for catering ideas, and the Directory for tent hire companies.

Tipis

Tipis and kata tents consist of a hand-crafted timber pole structure covered with natural canvas. The design allows for easy assembly and is intended to include a real fire in the centre. Giant Hat Kata tipis are huge and can be joined together to form beautiful arrangements with enough space for hundreds of guests. Hire companies can provide gorgeously rustic trestle tables and benches, which you can decorate with foliage and candles. During chilly evenings, lay vintage woollen or sheepskin blankets across the benches.

Wedding planner tip:
Ask guests to bring musical instruments with them to play when the band finishes.

Bedouin tents

The traditional, intricate design and colourfully printed canvas of Bedouin tents makes them a stunning backdrop. Hire companies can provide hand-painted wall panels, ceiling swags and embroidered floor cushions as well as furniture.

Yurts

Curvy and magical, yurts are a wonderful alternative to a marquee. These circular structures can be linked to form yurt villages, which can accommodate the largest wedding party. Separate yurts could have different functions, such as a 'bar' or 'chill-out' yurt. Choose low tables and floor cushions for a laid-back atmosphere.

Cruck marquees

These have a traditional English timber frame overlaid with natural cotton canvas. Ideal for smaller gatherings, they are usually open at the sides so are best chosen in months when the risk of rain is lower. The attractive structure is simply enhanced by pretty native flowers and flickering candlelight (www.cruckmarquee.co.uk).

Traditional marquees

Usually made from natural canvas, with scalloped pelmets and 'big top' peaks, these suit colourful, homemade bunting and candy-stripe ribbons. I've helped couples keep to a tight budget with a marquee by avoiding extras such as linings and carpets, and hiring trestle tables and chairs separately. With all of these tent options, always check what is included in the price.

Guest camping

Some venues, such as Huntstile Organic Farm (www.huntstileorganicfarm.co.uk), offer camping. You could set up a small field of tipis, or ask guests to bring their own tent. Small tipis dotted among trees look wonderful.

A wood-framed Cruck marquee
(www.cruckmarquee.co.uk).

Canvas tips

❖ Look for companies that use sustainably
sourced timber for their structures.

❖ Some hire companies are carbon neutral
and plant trees to offset their delivery miles.

❖ A timber dance floor will help your guests
to find their dancing feet.

❖ Wind fresh ivy around timber supports
for natural decoration.

❖ Lay blankets across straw bales for instant,
comfortable seating.

Heritage and historic buildings

It is possible to find remarkable, historic wedding venues that are also ethically sound. Many larger buildings cover their high maintenance costs by hosting weddings and celebrations, so your custom is helping to preserve them. Old buildings, constructed using traditional techniques, generally contain less embodied energy than their contemporary counterparts. However, draughty mansions are likely to use more power in their day-to-day running. Venues that have been sympathetically upgraded to high energy-saving standards give the best of both worlds.

Historic homes

Stately homes, and other historic houses, are often licensed for civil ceremonies, and many will oversee all elements of your day, providing staff and sometimes their own wedding planners. Frequently they have outstanding grounds and gardens. Think about choosing a venue owned by a charity, such as The National Trust (www.nationaltrust.org.uk), which supports architectural conservation. Wakehurst Place in Sussex, managed by The Royal Botanic Gardens at Kew (www.kew.org), includes an arboretum and the Millennium Seed Bank, with all profits going to its plant conservation programme.

Country house weddings

Country house parties, where you hire a whole grand house for a day or weekend (rather like renting a holiday cottage), have become highly fashionable. Generally you will have the place to yourself, and are responsible for arranging outside caterers, music and flowers, but check individual venues to see what they include. Look for those that have been carefully restored using environmentally responsible techniques.

Castles and follies

Castles are the ideal backdrop for a fairy-tale wedding. Some can accommodate your guests overnight, so cutting down on travel. Others, such as Thornbury Castle (www.thornburycastle.co.uk), have their own herb gardens and vineyards, so you can use their produce.

Small and intimate, follies range from miniature country houses to classical temples. A few are licensed for civil ceremonies, such as the Red House at Painswick Rococo Garden in Gloucestershire (www.rococogarden.org.uk). Team with a traditional marquee in nearby grounds.

Mills and barns

Brimming with rustic charm, mills have often been sympathetically converted, and may have a fully working water wheel and flour stones (so you can serve homemade bread using their flour). Winkworth Farm mill (www.winkworthfarm.com) has solar-powered hot water and a cut flower garden, too.

Barns can be small and unconverted, with straw on the floor, or grand architectural transformations. There are good examples to fit all budgets and sizes of wedding, and they are often licensed for marriages in the UK.

Church weddings

Ancient churches lit by candlelight can be one of the most romantic settings for your wedding ceremony. Fees vary, but all go towards the upkeep and maintenance of these historic buildings. Why not arrange to leave your flowers for the next service?

The grounds of Sheepdrove
Organic Farm in Berkshire.

Wedding planner tip:
Ask the owner of the park or garden if
you can pick a few flowers for your hair,
bouquet or buttonholes.

The great outdoors

For those who love being outdoors, there can be no better place to marry than in a garden or wood, or on a sandy beach. Riverbanks, arboretums and lakes all make wonderful settings, while marrying under a beautiful, ancient tree is intimate and romantic, with little environmental impact. Inclement weather can pose a problem, so look for venues with their own shelter, and select appropriate footwear.

For information on the legalities of marrying outdoors, see page 30.

Arboretums

Full of ancient trees, blossoming shrubs and wild flowers, for me arboretums are perfect venues. Many are happy to host weddings and have small buildings available for year-round celebrations, often built using their own timber. At Westonbirt Arboretum (www.forestry.gov.uk/westonbirt), the Oak Hall is licensed for weddings. Marry in springtime to take advantage of tree blossoms, or in autumn as the leaves change colour.

Botanical gardens

What could be better than strolling with your guests around a colourful, wildlife-filled floral garden? Botanical gardens often incorporate streams and boating lakes, and some have their own follies, ideal for a ceremony. Check with the gardens or the local authority if they allow weddings, and whether they are licensed.

Local parks

You may have a park near your home that you regularly visit through the seasons. Well-maintained and full of champion trees and specimen plants, parks can provide the ideal backdrop not only for photographs but also for a wedding party picnic. If you are marrying in a nearby church, why not host drinks in the park. You will need to ask permission from the local authority.

Wildlife conservation centres

These make an unusual and inspirational setting. Wildlife charities work hard to protect endangered species and habitats, and rehabilitate animals of all types. The London Wetland Centre, a wide-open space in the city, is licensed for civil ceremonies (www.wwt.org.uk). You could link your wedding list to you chosen centre and ask your guests to make a donation to their valuable work.

Beaches

A beach wedding party can be an ideal low-impact reception. With invigorating scenery, plenty of space for guests and fabulous photo opportunities, you and your friends will love it. Check for water quality at www.blueflag.org, make sure there are toilet facilities nearby, and always clear up thoroughly afterwards. Ask the local authority before you plan your event: some beaches allow campfires, but others have restrictions – on dogs, for example. You should also consider how your guests will travel to the beach, whether there are any hazards, and tide times (so you don't get stranded).

Going local

If you live in a house with a beautiful garden, or have friends or relatives who do, why go any further for your wedding party? It's a thrifty option, and environmentally friendly, as you can recycle as much as you like, and guests may be able to walk there. Encourage those travelling longer distances to use public transport or to car-share to reduce parking issues. You can easily obtain temporary marquee licences from your local authority – useful in case of rain. Remember to inform neighbours of your plans, to keep them happy, too. For more about setting up a garden party, see pages 23 and 159.

Finding a hall

Village halls and community centres are great for those on a tight budget. Many have on-site catering facilities, and provide a blank canvas ready for inventive decoration. Don't worry if you are not keen on the furniture; simply hire in different tables, chairs and linen to personalise your day. Village halls are often positioned next to churches and chapels. At one village hall reception we strung up floral bunting and laid a single flower on each napkin, and a couple of friends' sons acted as waiters and served the drinks.

Hiring what you need

Practically everything you will ever need for a wedding is available to hire. Try to choose natural materials, such as wooden tables and linen cloths. Local companies will mean lower transport distances. Appoint a trustworthy friend to unpack deliveries and supervise collection.

Available to hire

Tables, chairs, cushions, blankets, tablecloths and napkins, crockery and glassware, cutlery, bars, candelabras, vases, cakestands and cake knives.

Quick ways to transform your venue

With some imagination it is possible to convert the plainest of venues into a wedding wonderland. Work with what is already there, not against it, for the best results. See the Directory for suppliers.

❊ Hire in different furniture – choose trestle tables and benches to make best use of space.

❊ Cover unsightly tables with tablecloths made from unbleached cotton, natural linen or vintage fabrics.

❊ Use plant-wax candles and lanterns to light the room (check they are allowed).

❊ Hire chair covers to disguise tired chairs.

❊ Personalise the toilets by providing your own natural soaps and washes.

❊ Use flowers creatively to divert attention away from less attractive elements.

❊ Put up small handmade signs to direct your guests.

❊ Use fabric drapes to cover unappealing wall features.

❊ Choose candles naturally scented with essential oils to help the room smell fresh.

❊ Bring your iPod for the music.

❊ Hire in mismatched vintage crockery for retro chic.

❊ When choosing flower decorations, complement or incorporate a colour that is already in the room.

❊ Hang homemade bunting outside or inside to brighten up a dull colour scheme.

Chair decoration

This decoration was made with fresh lavender, as it was in season at the time, though dried lavender also looks lovely. I find gingham ribbon works particularly well, but you could use whatever suits your style.

You can use these decorations for the bride and groom's seats, or to show the seating places for close family. Alternatively, this type of decoration works beautifully for pew ends in a church.

FOR EACH CHAIR YOU WILL NEED:

45 lavender stems

1m of 2cm-wide gingham or other ribbon

30cm of 1cm-wide matching ribbon

Twine

Florist's shears or garden scissors

Fabric scissors

METHOD:

1. Take two lavender stems and cross one over the other just below the flower.
2. Cross a third stem over the second and keep going until you have 15 stems all crossed.
3. Put the bunch aside and repeat until you have three matching bunches.
4. Take one bunch and carefully add a second to the side. Repeat with the third bunch.
5. Check the symmetry and make sure that all the stems are crossing each other in the same direction.
6. Pull some of the stems lower to create a fuller effect.
7. Tie the bunch together securely under the flowers with a short piece of twine. Knot, and trim the ends off the twine.
8. Checking the size of the decoration against your chosen chair, use the shears to cut the ends off the bunch so that they are level.
9. Place the thinner ribbon behind the bunch vertically and tie it on with the wider ribbon.
10. Wrap the wider ribbon around the bunch a couple of times and fasten in a bow.
11. Trim the ends of the ribbon into small V-shapes with the fabric scissors, in line with the bottoms of the stems.
12. Tie on to your chosen chair.

Wedding planner tip:
Instead of lavender, you could use dried wheatsheaves for a rural feel, or for a harvest-time wedding.

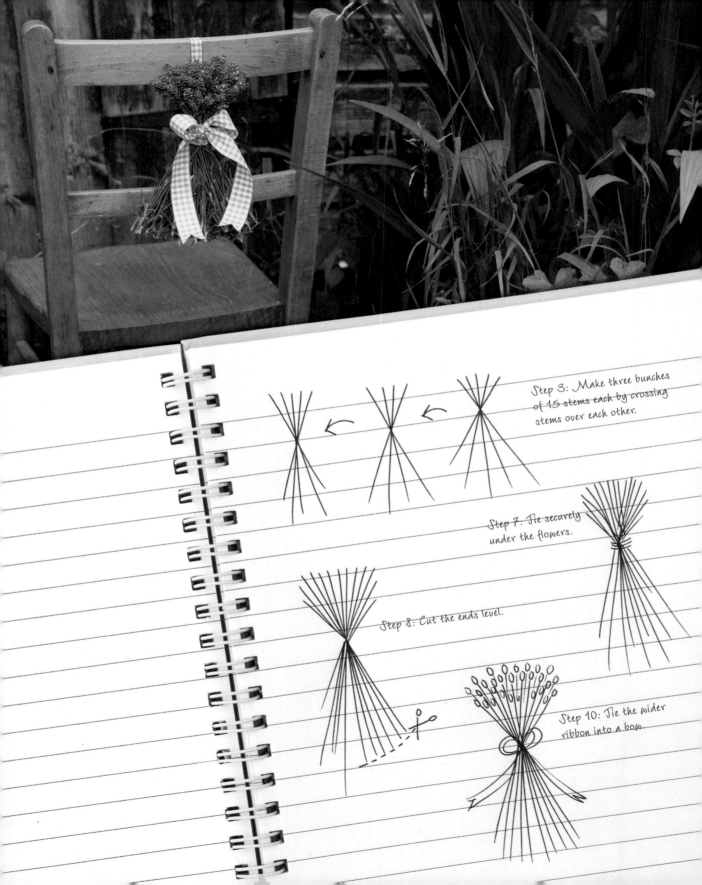

Step 3: Make three bunches of 15 stems each by crossing stems over each other.

Step 7: Tie securely under the flowers.

Step 8: Cut the ends level.

Step 10: Tie the wider ribbon into a bow.

❋ *How to choose the perfect dress*
Flattering your body shape.

❋ *Beautiful vintage gowns*
From 1920s chiffon to funky 1970s.

❋ *Charity chic*
Ethical dresses for the thrifty bride.

❋ *New and ethical*
The new designer trend and shopping advice.

❋ *Handmade and DIY*
Working with dressmakers and eco fabrics.

❋ *Revive that dress*
Heirloom gowns and a simple corsage.

❋ *Shoes, veils and trains*
Heirloom lace and eBay stilettos.

❋ *Grooms and bridesmaids*
Creating a stunning group effect.

The Dress

The dress is probably the most important and exciting of all your wedding purchases and places you centre stage. It is essential that you are comfortable in your choice, not only physically (you want to be able to breathe and sit down on you big day), but emotionally, too. This chapter suggests many fabulous, stylish and unusual options, so relax, take your time and enjoy finding your perfect gown.

Choosing your style

Step beyond the traditional shop-bought gown and you'll find many exciting alternatives. Svelte 1960s lace-covered shifts won on eBay, froths of chiffon from specialist vintage suppliers, gowns lovingly handmade in peace silk, floaty organic cotton maxi dresses worn with flower-woven hair. An heirloom gown reworked to fit perfectly, or a designer sample donated to a charity. All of them special; and they won't cost the earth.

Most wedding books will tell you to start shopping with your budget figure in mind, but this may mean you end up spending exactly that amount, and discounting other avenues because the dresses are below your budget. The easiest way to begin is by thinking about your wedding style and the season, and how you would like to feel on the day.

Your wedding notebook

Armed with your answers to the questions on the notepaper, below left, you should be able to focus more closely on your perfect dress type. At this stage it is useful to keep a small notebook, and clip or paste in any pictures, cards, fabric samples or sketches that you feel could be useful when choosing a dress (see the wedding notebook on page 32). Keep photos of flowers, venues and accessories, too – they will all help to give a feeling of your day and enable you to choose a dress that will fit with your vision.

Starting with your dress

Your dress can influence the whole style of your wedding. So if you dream of an elegant, minimalist reception, look for simple, classic cuts. For an intimate city wedding for two, set off a film-star vintage pencil skirt suit with a vibrant corsage. Think about colours, textures, fabrics and shape.

For a seasonally inspired look, you could choose your dress to complement your flowers – something delicate for cottage garden sweetpeas, or sumptuous velvet to go with winter blooms and rich foliage.

Natural options

Luckily there are many different dress avenues open to you, from gorgeous eco-friendly fabrics, to vintage dresses to die for. Feel free to mix it up! It's your day and your chance to shine.

What kind of dress do you imagine?

❈ How would you like to feel on the day – elegant, glamorous, dramatic, like a princess?

❈ What style do you imagine for your wedding (see Chapter 1)?

❈ What time of year is your wedding – chilly winter or hot summer?

❈ What type of ceremony are you having – outdoor, church, informal?

❈ How involved would you like to be in the creation of your dress?

❈ Do you want to be able to wear the gown again?

Wedding planner tip:
Brilliant pure white is a difficult colour to wear. Ivory, cream and ecru are generally more flattering.

The dress for your shape

You may have your eye on the perfect dress, but don't be afraid to step out of your comfort zone and try styles you would usually run a mile from – one of them could surprise you.

A-line

Elegant, with a fitted bodice and flared but structured skirt. Usually floor length. Suits most body shapes but may swamp more petite brides. Good if you have larger hips or are pear-shaped, as it skims out from the waist.

Empire line

Classic Jane Austen, fitted to under the bust, then falling in soft drapes. Especially lovely in floaty fabrics. Good for small-busted and petite brides, and comfortable with a pregnancy bump.

Prom style

Think 1950s, with a nipped-in waist, strapless or boat-neck bodice and full skirt to the knees or floor. Perfect for curvy girls, this style flatters larger hips, bottoms and thighs.

Bias cut

Glamorous and figure-skimming. Look to the 1930s for inspiration. Can be difficult to wear in a slinky fabric, but forgiving in a stiffer material. Good for tall girls and those who want to show off their curves.

Vintage gowns

Vintage, heirloom and second-hand dresses (sometimes known as 'preloved' or 'loved for longer') are perfect for girls who, like me, enjoy rummaging in antique and charity shops. They can be altered or embellished to suit your body shape and personality, and are often one of a kind. Strictly speaking, vintage covers the 1920s to 1960s, with pre-1920s classed as antique and 1970s onwards as retro.

The dress Sophie is wearing in the top picture on page 58 is an early 1960s cream lace straight shift with an elegant high neck, which I bought a few years ago on eBay, simply because I fell in love with it. The dress cost less than £20, including the postage, and arrived boxed, in perfect condition, complete with details of its happy history.

Where to buy

❉ Specialist vintage clothing shops and fairs in your area.

❉ eBay and other online auctions.

❉ Markets.

❉ Jumble and car-boot sales (you would be amazed!).

❉ Websites such as www.freudianslipsvintage.com (see the Directory for more).

Buying a vintage dress

Specialist vintage shops can give invaluable advice. An expert can tell you if a dress is easy to alter or too fragile to dance in. They should also be able to date your find and may even offer an insight into its history. Bear in mind that you do pay a premium for this level of service. While it's possible to find good vintage dresses for next to nothing, rare examples can cost the same as, or even more than, a new designer dress.

Get to know the shops you are visiting, as prices will vary. Research your subject so you know what you are looking at and the likely value. It can be helpful to take an honest (but open-minded) friend or relative – and remember that hems can be shortened, and embellishments added to cover the odd imperfection. Vintage dress sizes come up about two sizes smaller than modern equivalents. This explains why, although Marilyn Monroe is reported to have been a size 14, her dresses look tiny. Browse the online dress rails at www.londonvintageweddingfair.co.uk for inspiration.

An alternative is second-hand modern dresses, which can be cheaper and in better condition. We found Lisa's pink dress on page 187 at The Frock Exchange in Bath.

Online tips

Good measuring is the secret to buying when you can't try on. Check the waist, hips, bust, shoulder width, overall length and sleeve length. Then compare these with a dress that fits you well.

Ask questions of the seller. Does the zip work? Are there any visible marks or moth holes? Does the dress have any odours? You can always ask for extra photographs.

Opting for recorded delivery will help to ensure your gown arrives as promised.

Wedding planner tip:
Look online for wonderful vintage designer dress patterns — they cost a fraction of the price of a designer-label gown.

Decades of style

1920s The flapper dress

Skirt lengths rose daringly high (for the time) and bodices were short-sleeved or sleeveless. This was an age of elaborate decoration and fine fabrics: tiny glass beads and metallic threads combined with crêpe-de-chine, satin and taffeta.

1930s Age of glamour

Slender waistlines, long skirts and long sleeves, often in satin. The backless, bias-cut evening gown created a silhouette favouring slim hips and wider shoulders. Accessorised with boleros and small capes.

1940s War-time utility ▶

Dresses were well-proportioned and made to last. Silk was banned during the war, as it was needed for parachutes. Embellishments included covered buttons and sequins, which were freely available.

50s Prom queens ▶

ped-in waist and big, circular preferably with a full underskirt. ces were usually strapless and with elegant, elbow-length es and strings of pearls.

1960s The mini

The style was boyish, with straight-cut mini shift dresses teamed with block heels and glossy patent leather. Decoration was minimal for the modern look.

1970s Boho style ▶

After the geometric tailoring of the 1960s came the long, flowing lines of the maxi dress, with extended angel or bell sleeves. A fluid, romantic look decorated with strings of beads and daisy appliqué.

1980s Anything goes

Many different styles emerged, from punk to Victoriana, with wedding dress styles following high-street fashion. The quintessential 1980s dress had a full skirt and was heavily decorated with frills, ruffles, puff sleeves and lace.

Charity chic

Charity shops have become increasingly popular in recent years, as fashionable celebrities frequent their local branch looking for treasures. This new awareness has brought more competition for bargains, but also means there is a wider choice of donations, including higher-priced items. Most charity shops will stock wedding dresses from time to time, but it's worth visiting often, as stock may change daily. Ask friendly sales assistants if they can let you know when a wedding dress has come in.

Designer samples

The same rules apply to charity shopping as to vintage shopping, but if you have qualms about a second-hand dress, you'll be pleased to hear that many gowns donated to larger charities are either unworn, end-of-season stock, or catwalk samples given by designers. The dress pictured on the bottom left of this page still had its tags, and was a fraction of the price it would have been in a designer shop. Re-using a dress or accessory is the ultimate in recycling, and will help your budget, too.

Charity shops are also an Aladdin's cave of affordable accessories: everything from sparkly brooches and beaded tiaras to pretty vintage wraps and shoes. After the wedding you can always donate items back to the shop.

Oxfam Bridal

Oxfam has a number of specialist bridal departments in the UK, stocking hundreds of fabulous dresses. Their prices will please the thriftiest of brides-to-be, and with the proceeds going to charity, it really is the most ethical choice. These bridal departments also stock jewellery, shoes, veils, bridesmaids' dresses, page-boy and flower-girl outfits and menswear. With huge mirrors, generous fitting rooms and relaxed, friendly staff, you can not only have fun but find a dress to impress, too.

My charity shopping tips

❊ Try to be open-minded, and prepared to wait. You may discover the dress of your dreams on your first visit, but you may have to return several times to spot new arrivals.

❊ If you find a dress that seems perfect but is too big, don't despair. Most dresses can be altered to fit. If in doubt, ask the assistant to reserve the dress for you, and go back with an experienced seamstress to advise on alterations.

❊ Chances are there will only be one of each dress style, so if you fall in love with a gown, either buy or reserve it straight away.

❊ Charity shopping, like vintage shopping, is all about being unique. So dare to be different, accessorise with flair and be yourself.

What to take with you

❋ Your wedding notebook with inspiration pictures.

❋ Camera (charity shops don't mind if you take photos).

❋ A pair of natural-coloured tights.

❋ A hair clip or hair-band to tie up your hair.

❋ Shoes of the height you want to wear on your big day.

❋ A good friend to help you in the changing room.

❋ Plenty of time…

All these dresses came from eBay and our local Oxfam Bridal. We took them to the park, and had some fun trying them on.

This hand-finished dress
by Jessica Charleston
is made from fine
natural silk.

New dresses

When buying new, there are fortunately now many designer brands that take ethics and the environment seriously. We love these labels and have listed some in the Directory. You could also try www.greenunion.co.uk or www.ethicaljunction.org. Garments made in good humanitarian conditions tend to cost more, but you can find beautiful fairtrade silk and cotton gowns you will love.

Tammam, for example, uses organic and fairtrade materials, peace silks and vintage trimmings, and sells off-the-peg as well as bespoke gowns. Alternatively, find a maxi dress or a suit from an ethical designer, through ethical shopping sites such as www.ascensiononline.com, and add wedding touches with your accessories. Or try the amazing deconstructed garments at www.junkystyling.co.uk, where you can take in your old dresses to be reworked into something unique. Also check the guide to eco-friendly fabrics on page 64.

Shopping ethically

Not all bridal shops advertise where their dresses are made or the conditions for workers there. Some mainstream brands are manufactured in China so have chunky carbon footprints.

Many companies understand it is not acceptable to use child labour or pay below a minimum wage, and are making efforts to source their clothes more ethically, but unfortunately bad practices still exist. It can be argued that developing countries need the employment provided by western economies, but some employees are expected to endure unacceptable conditions and communities may be exposed to toxic substances, such as the pesticides used to grow fibre crops.

My advice would be to ask where your garment has been manufactured. If you are keen on a particular brand, ask to see their ethics statement. You can also check manufacturers at www.ethiscore.org.uk.

Wedding fairs

People often dismiss wedding fairs, but they can be a great way to discover small, family-run companies that manufacture locally, and up-and-coming designers of dresses, accessories and wedding decorations who use natural and vintage materials. Many designers will sell their samples or discontinued stock and may offer a special exhibition discount. If you are prepared to decide on the spot you could save a small fortune. Go wearing neutral underwear, pack a hair-band and your notebook, and take your mum or a friend. It can be a bit of a scrum, but try not to impulse buy because you feel pressured.

Bridal shops

Some bridal shops are wonderful, will expertly fit a sample dress to your frame, and choose the perfect accessories and bridal underwear to complete the picture. Others, however, will dictate which dresses you are 'allowed' to try, will tut under their breath and generally make you feel uncomfortable. If you are looking for an ethical dress or natural fabrics such as silk, do ask questions, and feel free to visit and try on a dress more than once. Ask how many fittings are required, and say when you would like the final one. There may be charges for delivery and storage.

Wedding planner tip:
I always recommend that brides sit down in a dress they are trying. Is it still comfortable?

Handmade and homemade

A handmade dress is a wonderful luxury, when it's thoughtfully designed and made to fit you perfectly. Think about choosing an eco or vintage fabric (see page 64). Handmade doesn't have to be expensive. Making your own wedding gown is completely possible if you have good sewing skills and the time. A reasonably simple pattern will be less stressful. Or you could ask a friend or relative – although remember that you may have to request alterations if there are details you don't like, and you may find this awkward. The main cost will be the fabric, which can prove expensive.

If your ideal dress is elaborate, then a specialist dressmaker may be the wisest choice. Whichever route you decide on, have your wedding notebook to hand, with pictures, samples of fabric and other inspirations, to make sure that everyone understands your 'dream dress' vision.

Home sewing

Before buying your pattern it helps to try on ready-made dresses in differing styles so you know what suits you. With your pattern, first make up a 'toile' in a cheaper fabric such as natural calico (or an old bed sheet), so you can adjust the fit and details.

Alternatively, use a dress from your wardrobe that you love as a template. You will have to cut your own pattern, but this is not difficult and most sewing classes can teach you how. Alternatively, a good dressmaker could do this for you. For hints and tips on all things sewing, www.burdastyle.com is the website to visit.

Vintage patterns

These are available through the same outlets as vintage dresses (see the Directory); patterns are inexpensive and easily customised.

Before you buy a vintage pattern:
* Check that all parts of the pattern are included.
* If the pattern has already been cut (not necessarily a problem), make sure it has been cut to your size or larger.
* Double-check measurements, not just the dress size, as vintage sizes are smaller.

Tips for working with a dressmaker

❊ A wedding dress is incredibly personal, so it is important that you click with your dressmaker. Choose someone through a recommendation and meet them in person before committing.

❊ As with any professional, ask for a detailed written quotation and time estimate, follow up references or testimonials, and get a receipt for any deposits you pay.

❊ Study photographs and samples of their handiwork to check the workmanship on details such as seams.

❊ If you have a particular eco fabric in mind, or want only natural or vintage embellishments, ensure they are agreeable to this approach.

❊ A good dressmaker will be able to advise you on what styles will flatter your body shape, so listen to their opinion.

❊ If you don't like something about the dress as it is progressing, tell your dressmaker. They are not mind readers, but they do want you to love your dress.

The Makery is one of the new breed of craft workshop spaces where you can have fun learning new sewing skills (www.themakeryonline.co.uk).

Eco fabrics

Designers and producers are bringing us a growing range of gorgeous fabrics that are gentler on our skin and on the environment. Many are a fresh twist on long-loved natural fibres. For suppliers see the Directory on page 208.

Peace silk (vegetarian or wild crafted silk)

Silk is a completely natural product made from the cocoon of the silk worm. It is wonderfully light and breathable. However, traditional silk is harvested by boiling the cocoons and killing the worms before they hatch, which may offend some people.

When a silk worm hatches, it makes a hole in the end of the cocoon, breaking the continuous silk thread. With peace silk the worms are allowed to hatch, and the fabric is made with the cocoon remnants. The resulting material is slightly rougher than regular silk but still beautiful. It is rarer and more expensive.

Hemp and hemp silk

Hemp is a relatively new material for wedding dresses, although it has been used in day-to-day clothing for many years. Environmentally friendly, hemp cloth is soft to touch, although with a slightly grainy appearance. It is often blended with silk to give a soft-sheen, satiny fabric that is lovely for special lingerie. Hemp grows quickly and easily even in wet climates, and doesn't need fertilisers or spraying with insecticides.

Bamboo

A soft and smooth natural fabric that drapes well, almost like silk. Bamboo grass doesn't need fertilisers, grows quickly and absorbs vast amounts of carbon dioxide. The fabric does not wrinkle easily, has natural anti-bacterial properties and is a safer option for sensitive skins. Natural organic, unbleached bamboo is a flattering creamy colour.

Organic cotton

Cotton is often overlooked as a celebration dress fabric, but can be gorgeous stitched with lace and is perfectly light and cool in summer. Most cotton is heavily sprayed with pesticides, so choose organic and fairtrade where possible. For pure whites look for eco-bleached cotton.

Linen

You probably already have some linen in your wardrobe. Made from the flax plant, it is fairly labour intensive to process, hence its high price. Linen is a great choice for summer, as it is so cool to wear – but beware the dreaded linen wrinkles.

Nettle

Some may balk at the thought of using stinging nettles for their wedding dress, but they make a fabulous fabric with a slightly silky feeling. The fibre is often blended with organic cotton. Nettles are environmentally friendly plants, growing abundantly in damp, temperate climates.

Natural dyes

Modern natural vegetable dyes, and instructions on getting the best results from them, are available online. You could transform any of the eco fabrics mentioned here to a colour of your choice: either dye the whole dress, or just one element, such as a sash or corsage. Vegetable dyes come in an exciting range of colours, but if you feel unsure about dying the fabric yourself, buy it ready dyed. For more information look at www.greenfibres.com.

Vintage and reclaimed materials

A handmade dress in vintage fabric will give you a gown that's unique, and with a low carbon footprint, as the material has already been used once. You may have a trunk of fabrics and trimmings in your attic, but if not, you can find these in charity shops, vintage costume stores and online. You could also use material from an existing wedding dress – great if you have an heirloom or eBay dress and adore the fabric but not the style.

Think about remnants from fabric stores, too: there is minimal expenditure and you're making use of a resource that might otherwise have been thrown away.

But remember that a wedding gown uses considerably more material than a regular dress. Embellishments such as ribbons, buttons and bows can all be given a fresh lease of life as part of a new gown.

Wedding planner tip:
Use a vintage dress pattern with a contemporary eco fabric for a chic, individual look.

Dresses for free and cleaning

A free wedding dress...? The idea will probably come as a surprise to most brides, but searching for a free dress can turn into an exciting challenge. Freecycle is a free-to-join online community where members post notices about unwanted items and ask for things they need. Do a search to find your local Freecycle or similar community. You may get lucky and find an 'OFFER: Wedding Dress', but you will almost certainly have to put up a 'Wanted' post. Personalise this request, as the potential giver will want to know their special dress is destined for a good home. Freecycle is full of wonderful people, but like all online resources it can be victim to the occasional bad penny, so be sensible when going to collect.

Something borrowed

Swishing parties have become something of a craze. Essentially they are clothes-swapping events, where you take your lovely-but-no-longer-worn items to give away and hopefully bag a few choice pieces to revive your wardrobe. You are unlikely to find the wedding dress of your dreams, but may discover the perfect accessory, or even a white day dress or beaded evening gown.

How about borrowing from a friend? Most brides keep their dress for a couple of years at least. Don't let age fool you, either: your mum's best friend may have the perfect vintage dress hiding in her wardrobe. Check that it fits, and that the owner doesn't mind if you make alterations.

Heirloom gowns

You may be the lucky inheritor of an heirloom wedding dress, passed down from your mother or even your grandmother. Don't discount it because it is not your style: most dresses, even 1980s meringues, can be reworked, although you may need a seamstress. Alternatively, just reclaim the fabric and trimmings.

To hire or not to hire

Gowns that would cost thousands of pounds new can be hired for a fraction of the price, and the fact that a hired dress is worn a number of times makes it a potentially eco-friendly option. However, the dresses will be dry-cleaned each time they are worn. If you have sensitive skin or are worried about the chemicals used, ask exactly how the shop cleans the dresses and if they use a more environmentally friendly cleaning process.

Cleaning and storage

Dresses should always be cleaned immediately after wearing and before you store them, as perspiration discolours over time. While some modern dresses are machine or hand-washable, others are dry clean only, especially if they have beading or decorative touches. If a vintage gown looks clean but smells musty, hang it in a steamy bathroom for a couple of days. The steam will also help any creases drop out.

Some specialists can dry-clean your dress immaculately without the toxic chemicals used in regular dry-cleaning. One option is called the GreenEarth process (www.greenearthcleaning.com). This is becoming increasingly widespread. These dry cleaners are also the best place to buy an acid-free box and tissue to store your precious gown (remember to pad out the bodice with tissue if it is boned).

Covering marks

If marks refuse to disappear, you can always cover them up. First try a little chalk. This is a good emergency trick for marks discovered on the big day and will cover a blemish on most shades of white. Or hide the mark with an accessory, such as a corsage or brooch, or even a scarf. They will never know! See the box opposite for more ideas to add a fresh spark or personalise your dress.

Revive that dress

❋ Tie a wide satin ribbon in a contrasting colour simply at the waist as a sash. Choose a hue to match your flowers, such as cornflower blue, or velvety purple tulip. Fasten with a sparkly vintage brooch.

❋ Pin a large flower corsage at the collarbone. Corsages are easy to make, so you could have a girly day with your bridesmaids creating accessories for your wedding (see page 68).

❋ Remove 1980s puff sleeves and net underskirts to transform a retro dress into a simpler, sleeveless silhouette.

❋ Shorten a dress that is too long and use the extra fabric to make a matching wedding day bag.

❋ If a dress you love is too short, consider lengthening it with a fabric in a matching colour but with a contrasting texture, or be daring and add fabric in a complementary colour.

Emma's dress is a simple beaded 1920s-style chiffon. We added a vintage dress clip and drop earrings, with a corsage to match her colouring.

Fabric flower corsage

This corsage is easy to make in about an hour. You can use as many layers of fabric as you wish — the more layers, the more elaborate the finished corsage will be. For those shown in the photograph on the right, I used a vintage silk slip combined with organic cotton.

YOU WILL NEED:

Natural fabrics such as silk, hemp or organic cotton

Reclaimed netting from underskirts

Fabric scissors

Needle, pins and matching thread

Piece of paper

Vintage buttons or a vintage brooch

Brooch back

METHOD:

1. Cut a circle of fabric 10cm in diameter, another in a different fabric 9cm in diameter and a third 6cm in diameter. Cut two pieces of netting, one 9cm in diameter and one 6cm in diameter.

2. Take the largest two fabric circles and place the larger netting circle on top. Secure together with a small stitch in the centre.

3. On a rectangle of paper measuring 10cm by 5cm draw the shape shown on the notebook opposite and cut out.

4. Cut out a rectangle of fabric 10cm by 10cm and fold in half. Pin on the paper template and cut out. If using silk, after cutting, gently pull the edges at a diagonal, for a 'fluted' effect. Repeat 4 times.

5. Fold each fabric shape diagonally across once, then again, to make a quarter. The edges should *not* line up.

6. Take two of the quarters and overlap them slightly, securing with three small stitches. Overlap the other two quarters similarly and stitch to secure.

7. Place your 'circle' of quarters in the centre of your larger circle of three fabrics, then layer the smaller fabric and net circles on top.

8. Position your button in the centre and sew together.

9. Cut one final circle of fabric 3cm in diameter. Take a brooch back and sew this securely through the tiny circle on to the corsage.

10. Fluff up the petals and enjoy.

Wedding planner tip:
The measurements are for the smaller corsage shown. To make a larger one, simply increase the sizes of fabric circles.

Step 4: Use the paper pattern to cut out your folded fabric.

This is the fabric shape you need to cut out.

Step 5: Fold your shape in half diagonally . . .

. . . and then again to make a quarter.

Step 6: Overlap the quarters and stitch.

Step 8: Layer your corsage and sew the button through.

Shoes, veils and trains

It's often assumed that brides will wear white satin heels, but most of us don't have any use for this kind of shoe after the day. How about silver or gold sparkly sandals, or even flip-flops, instead? Or invest in two pairs (affordable if they come from a charity shop): the killer heels for the ceremony and a comfortable pair for dancing. If you choose something you really like – not just to go with the dress – you'll be more likely to wear them again.

Embellishing shoes can be surprisingly enjoyable: pin on corsages or brooches, or glue on beads and sequins to give a wedding lift (but remember that less is more with decorations). I worked with a bride once who wore a formal floor-length gown, but glimpsed beneath, when she lifted her skirt, were a pair of pretty white shoes with crisscrossing blue ribbons. She had carefully stitched on the ribbons to mimic ballet slippers, and tied them in a decorative bow. The ribbon was vintage, so it was her something old as well as her something blue – and it added an element of surprise to her traditional outfit.

Depending on the time of year and where you are marrying, I would also recommend taking along a pair of wellies. You can then go striding around the lake for amazing photographs with your new husband.

Veils

Some brides cannot imagine their wedding outfit without a veil, while others dread the thought. It also depends on your dress – a gold sparkly cocktail dress wouldn't take a veil, for example. The usual guideline is that veils look best with white, ivory or cream. The question of veil length is a minefield, but a good rule of thumb is the longer the dress, the longer the veil.

If you are lucky enough to have inherited a veil from a family member it would be lovely to include this heirloom in your day. You can also find vintage veils, and with a little patience you can make your own. Veils that are too long can easily be shortened with a few basic sewing skills (or by a seamstress). Similarly, you can buy a plain veil and add panache by sewing on small glass beads or ribbons. This could take a few hours but will save you a small fortune. Look at embroidery books – the older the better – for unusual patterns; search on Amazon for ideas.

Tips for choosing a veil
* Consider your dress colour, style and length.
* Do you want to be able to remove the veil after the ceremony, or would you like to keep it on for the reception and dancing?
* Think about contrasting fabrics, such as lace.
* Are you going to be wearing your hair up or down?
* What time of year are you marrying? Veils can be quite a handful in gusty winds!

A quick word on trains

Generally speaking, the more formal the wedding, the longer the train – although if you yearn to wear a gown with a ten-foot-long train on the beach, why not?

Make sure that you or a friend know how to 'bustle up' the train (wedding speak for tying it up under the gown so you can dance without tripping over). Long trains can he held off the floor with a thumb loop that hooks around your thumb or middle finger, allowing you to swish around elegantly.

Wedding planner tip:
Always wear in new shoes before the wedding and scuff the soles to ensure comfy feet and no slip-ups on the day.

Grooms and bridesmaids

Grooms can be adventurous, ethical and eco-chic, and enjoy being in the spotlight alongside their bride. It helps if your bride and groom outfits are in sync. With a groom in top hat and tails the bride really needs a fabulous floor-length gown, but if you are wearing a short silk shift dress, then he should be in a suit and tie. Think about coordinating the colour of your bouquet or sash to his tie, cravat or suit lining. You could even have fabrics or handkerchiefs dyed to match with natural vegetable dyes.

Natural fabrics

In summer there's nothing more comfortable than a linen suit. It allows the skin to breathe, keeping the wearer cool. Remember linen can crease and looks better in a lighter colour. Men's shirts can also be found in the natural fabrics listed on page 64. Hemp and organic cotton both look and feel great and are readily available.

Vintage groom

Your fiancé may have an heirloom suit hidden away, but if not, men's vintage shops are starting to spring up. Vintage or retro style – think 1950s pinstripes and wide shoulders, or Sean Connery slimline 1960s suits – has become a fashionable look for grooms. As well as second-hand, you could also look at vintage-inspired styles such as floral patterned shirts.

Wedding planner tip:
Find ties, shoes and cufflinks in charity shops. Or translate the tradition of wearing something borrowed to the groom.

Hired groomswear

Hiring a suit is popular with grooms as it's easy and costs less – especially with formal options such as morning dress. For a large wedding, with many ushers and groomsmen, hiring is the perfect way to make sure the bridal party all match. If the groom wants to stand out, he could buy a colourful cravat, tie or shirt to personalise his outfit. Pedro's outfit on page 187 is from www.mossbros.co.uk.

Splashing out

Once in a while a groom will have a suit handmade for his big day. A lovely idea, and green, too, if the suit can be worn again. He could choose a lining in a bright colour, perhaps to match your sash or corsage. Why not opt for an eco fabric, such as linen, or an organic or vintage wool weave, and complement it with an unusual vintage lining.

Bridesmaids

Most of the advice in this chapter also applies to bridesmaids' outfits. For a formal wedding the usual 'rule' is that the bridesmaids should match the bride in some way, or at least each other. But if you are a free spirit, why not let your bridesmaids choose their own dresses?

I attended a wedding where the bridesmaids wore bright, floral, 1970s-style frocks, not at all in keeping with the bride. But it looked amazing. If bridesmaids make their own choice, chances are they will wear the outfit again, making it more environmentally friendly.

With page boys and flower girls the advice is simple: make sure they are comfortable. For girls, ballet slippers are the best footwear. Flower girls like to have accessories to make them feel special, such as baskets of fresh flower petals. Little boys are typically not fussed!

- ❋ Heirloom finds and second-hand jewels
  How to wear them and where to buy.

- ❋ Cleaner gold and ethical diamonds
  What every girl needs to know,
  plus wooden rings.

- ❋ Buttons, beads and flowers
  Unusual alternatives to traditional
  wedding jewellery.

- ❋ Boleros, wraps, scarves and corsages
  From vintage sequins to chunky knits.

- ❋ Eco-friendly underwear
  Stunning handmade corsets and
  soft, hemp-silk camisoles.

- ❋ Wedding day bags
  A guide to styles, embellishing, and a chic,
  make-your-own bag.

Accessories

Choosing all the little bits and pieces to go with your
dress – the bags and earrings and bracelets – can be
such fun. Rummaging in vintage shops and antique
markets with your friends; discovering artisan
makers and modern eco designers who'll craft
something special. Personally, I can't resist searching
out something unusual, and this chapter has plenty
of ideas so you can find your dream accessories, too.

Creative places to find your jewellery

Shimmering sea-glass beads and intricate Victorian earrings, heirloom gold bands or sleek, modern minimalism. It's surprisingly easy to find a wealth of eco-chic accessories, whatever your budget and personal style. There are plenty of alternatives, from online ethical stores to charity shops, recycling, borrowing, or making your own (see the Directory).

Take a picture of your dress or a cutting of the fabric to markets and shops, and remember Coco Chanel's advice: "When accessorising, always take off the last thing you put on."

Heirloom finds

You may be lucky enough to have an heirloom piece from a relative. If it is faultless you could wear it conventionally, or think about imaginative ways to show it off. Pin a brooch on to a waistband, use as a hair accessory, or to decorate a bag. Dress clips make fabulous shoe embellishments and long necklaces can be wound around several times for a more modern feel.

If an item is damaged, don't rule out having it mended by your local jeweller, or ask them to rework it into something more wearable. Stones can be salvaged and re-used to make a completely different piece.

Antique gems

High-quality antique jewellery is an investment, but often costs only a fraction of the price of a new piece and, being second-hand, is effectively carbon neutral.

You'll find geometric art deco rings, Edwardian marcasite brooches, Victorian hat pins and Georgian glass necklaces in specialist antique jewellery shops and markets, or at auctions by www.christies.com or www.bonhams.com – and they won't all cost a fortune. Online, browse www.alfiesantiques.com and www.steptoesantiques.co.uk. Pre-1940 jewellery is classed as antique, later as vintage.

Hallmarks on precious metals will tell you details of the quality, age and where the item was made. The Miller's antiques guides are helpful if you want to learn more.

Vintage costume jewellery

Vintage jewellery is one of my favourite things and is easily found in flea markets, antique fairs and charity shops. Try www.vintagefair.co.uk, www.manhattanvintage.com or www.lovevintage.com.au, depending on where you live. Raid your grandmother's or mother's jewellery boxes (with their permission, of course); they may have beautiful necklaces or brooches squirreled away that will look fresh and modern when teamed with the right dress.

Charity shops

These can be a rich source of inexpensive accessories, especially if you are happy to revisit regularly to check for new donations. Styles range from long, wooden bead necklaces to delicate silver chains, lucite bangles, 1950s clip-on earrings and 1980s cocktail rings. Frequently they will be in immaculate, unworn condition. But even if a piece is broken or dusty, you can have it cleaned and repaired for minimal cost – so if you love it, take it home. Buying from charity shops is eco-friendly and ethical, too.

Markets and car-boot sales

These are a good place to find more modern second-hand designs. Go early to catch the bargains and remember that they will only have one of each item.

This vintage-inspired pendant is handmade by Jessie Chorley (www.jessiechorley.com). The bracelet opposite is artisan made from recycled tins.

Be different with jewellery
* Use over-sized vintage earrings as brooches.
* Antique charm bracelets can look really pretty.
* Marcasite is inexpensive and sparkly – perfect for a glamorous wedding.
* Use broken jewellery to make something new, such as a tiara.
* Embellish fabric corsages with small brooches for a touch of sparkle.

once upon a time

Ethical rings

The production of new gem stones can be damaging to the environment and sometimes the wellbeing of local communities, due to the invasive and chemical-laden extraction techniques. Unethical working practices are commonplace. Responsible jewellery designers are now realising that this is unacceptable and are re-using and recycling stones and metals where possible. You can also find beautiful fairtrade designs. See the Directory for jewellers we recommend.

Ethical diamonds

The issue of conflict (or blood) diamonds is now widely documented. Diamonds are still the preferred gem for engagement, wedding and eternity rings, so it is important to do your research and buy with care. Non-conflict diamonds that have been mined and exported under fairtrade and ethical conditions are widely available. But the only way to be certain where yours come from is to buy from a reputable dealer and check they have certification. The Kimberley Process runs an international certification scheme for rough diamonds, helping to prevent the trade in conflict gems.

The Diamond Council also has a System of Warranties whereby buyers and sellers of both rough and polished diamonds have to confirm that they are conflict-free and in compliance with United Nations resolutions. See www.greenkarat.com and www.diamondfacts.org.

Unfortunately, all diamond mining – even ethical production in countries such as Canada – causes environmental damage, simply due to the process. Synthetic diamonds are becoming more popular as an alternative and are said to be indistinguishable from mined diamonds. Whether this is a suitable replacement for a naturally occurring mineral is down to personal choice, although they are now considered to be the most ethically and environmentally aware option. Browse online at www.greenkarat.com and www.gemesis.com.

Cleaner gold and platinum

Gold and platinum extraction carries a high environmental price, as it uses chemicals such as mercury and cyanide. You can find cleaner gold and platinum, mined under better environmental and fairtrade conditions, although supply is currently limited. Ask your jeweller if they use these cleaner metals.

Both gold and platinum are highly recyclable and can be re-used to make rings and jewellery that appear new, with no further environmental impact. Look for artisans using post-consumer recycled gold and platinum.

You may have a piece of jewellery at home that could be melted down and made into a new ring. Some jewellers will happily do this for you, and encourage you to be involved in its design. A number of innovative companies hold workshops at their studios so that you can come in and help with the process of making the rings yourselves (see the Directory listings).

Wooden rings

These are a delightful ethical alternative to a metal ring and are skilfully crafted from native non-tropical hardwoods such as yew, oak and cherry. Completely natural, and warm to wear, wooden rings will last for years with the correct care. They often come presented in a matching wooden box. The rings pictured above are from www.wooden.co.uk, or see www.etsy.com.

> **Wedding planner tip:**
> Clean gem stones using an old soft toothbrush and eco washing-up liquid for sparkling results.

Beads for all occasions

Beads are always in fashion, whatever the season, and come in all manner of sizes, lengths, shapes and styles – see the tips opposite for ideas. They are easy to string yourself: look for courses to learn beading techniques and to gather inspiration. Try salvaging broken necklaces and using the beads to create something new.

Sea glass

Fragments of glass are naturally polished by the sea into smooth pebbles in shades of blue and aqua, foamy white, rich green and amber, and occasionally rare pink. Sea glass can be hundreds of years old and each piece is unique. Gina Cowen (www.seaglass.co.uk) makes magically beautiful sea jewels (see left and page 25).

Recycled beads

Look in galleries and online for inspiring artisans designing eco-friendly necklaces and bracelets with beads made from recycled glass beads. Brilliantly reflective and found in countless colours, they make stunning jewellery (see www.juzionline.com).

Buttons

Pretty vintage and antique buttons with intricate designs can be used in the same way as beads. Simply thread on to fine beading string (available from craft suppliers) so the buttons lie flat. Search out antique mother of pearl buttons, which gently reflect the light. Find vintage buttons at charity shops (they often cut them off damaged garments that are going to be recycled as textiles), online and at specialist antique market stalls.

Beaded tiaras

These are easy to make yourself – a workshop can be a fantastic alternative hen party. Use salvaged beads and recycled fine wire for a perfectly eco accessory. It's worth checking frequently in a mirror to make sure that your design suits your face shape.

Tips for wearing your beads

❋ Wooden beads are an environmentally sound choice if they are vintage or FSC accredited, and look fabulous with 1970s flowing gowns. Choose pale woods to suit a light-coloured dress.

❋ For a 1950s-themed wedding, accessorise with vintage, chunky-beaded necklaces in bold, primary colours.

❋ Delicate glass and crystal beads catch the light beautifully. Look out for antique strings for romantic simplicity.

❋ Antique pearls are timeless and will grace almost any outfit. Colours vary so choose carefully to complement both your dress and your skin tone.

Hair-bands and daisy chains

Hair-bands add interest with minimal effort, whether your hair is long or short. Simple to make from elastic or wire, they can be wound with fine ribbons and decorated with vintage corsages, bows and brooches, or fresh flowers.

Narrow fabric hair-bands are especially chic worn across the forehead with loose, flowing hair – perfect for a laid-back beach wedding. Decorate with small, fabric blooms and tiny beads for natural summer style.

We made impromptu daisy chains for our bride, Lisa, above, and our flower girls. Simple, beautifully effective and ideal for an informal country or garden wedding. Remember to make them at the last moment so they stay fresh.

Wedding planner tip:
The current trend is to wear either earrings or a necklace, but not both together.

Boleros and corsages

The accessories you choose can lift a plain dress or tie an outfit together. Try unusual combinations of colour, texture and layering, as we have in the photograph opposite. Boleros and wraps can be useful whether your wedding is in deep winter or high summer.

Boleros, which are cropped, mid-sleeved jackets, are smart and stylish as part of a skirt suit, or keep cold at bay worn over a dress in the winter months.

Fine silk wraps will shield bare arms from hot sunshine or add a layer of warmth in early spring and autumn. Knitted ballet wrap cardigans in creamy whites and soft pinks, finished with wide satin ribbon tie bows, add a twist to a traditional strapless dress.

Scarves

I always feel that scarves are an under-used wedding accessory, whether vintage silk or heavy knit. if your photographs are being taken in snow, a chunky white bobble scarf will add fashion-shoot glamour.

Gorgeous old silk scarves from vintage shops come in all sorts of patterns, colours and sizes. Larger ones can be used as a wrap, while the smaller ones look fabulous simply tied asymmetrically around the neck. This looks especially chic with a 1950s dress. You can even use men's brightly coloured silk hankies as scarves – vintage handkerchiefs are usually well made.

If you are having a dress made in an eco fabric such as hemp silk or raw peace silk, you could use the offcuts to make delicate scarves to match.

Wedding planner tip:
Update an existing wrap cardigan by swapping knitted ties for beautiful reclaimed satin ribbons.

Ribbons

Vintage ribbons in unusual colours and textures can make strikingly simple accessories. For an almost instant choker, hem the ends and attach a small piece of Velcro or a button fastening. A friend made a contrasting black and white choker like this as a last-minute necklace alternative before heading out as a wedding guest. You could try layering ribbons in different widths and tones, or sewing on a corsage, beads or buttons.

Corsages

Fresh flower and fabric corsages are in vogue, worn with jeans as well as wedding dresses. You could make your own from cream-toned eco fabrics, handmade felt, or brightly coloured offcuts of material (see page 68 for my simple method), or scout out vintage gems. If you find a fabric corsage that you adore but is in poor condition, give it a new lease of life by carefully taking it apart and reworking, adding extra fabrics and ribbons.

Using fresh flowers

Floral accessories have a minimal carbon footprint if the flowers have been grown locally.

❋ Fresh flower wrist corsages are the ultimate retro prom accessory. They can look wonderful, especially for an outdoor wedding – and you could give your bridesmaids smaller matching versions.

❋ Try attaching a single fresh flower to one side of a ribbon sash. Ask advice from your florist as you will need a relatively hardy species.

❋ Floral headdresses have recently come back into fashion. They work best with tiny seasonal blooms that complement your skin tone and dress.

Ways with corsages

* Fasten a beautiful antique corsage to a length of ribbon as a vintage-inspired choker.

* Wear a large fresh flower corsage in your hair.

* Oversized soft eco fabric corsages look fabulous attached to matching wide belts for urban eco-chic.

* Ask your dress designer for extra fabric to make your own corsage.

* Give your bridesmaids individual style with matching dresses but contrasting corsages.

This simple dress, shot at The Makery, is lifted by a matching 1940s corsage and ballet wrap, and a play-in-the-snow chunky knit scarf.

Hemp-silk camisole from
Jenny Ambrose at Enamore.

Camisoles and pretty underwear

Beautiful knickers made from hemp silk and vintage ribbons are a fabulous indulgence for a bride. Eco girls will love the soft organic bamboo or natural cotton ranges that are now available, complete with pretty lace trimmings. Look online at makers such as www.enamore.co.uk. Choose fairtrade for maximum ethical score, or make your own using vintage fabrics. Find easy patterns at www.burdastyle.com.

Perfect underwear

❖ Try your chosen underwear on with your dress, as sheer fabrics may reveal more than you bargained for.

❖ Ivory or nude-coloured underwear is best under white, ivory and champagne dresses. With a strong-coloured dress such as red, you could team your underwear accordingly.

❖ Splash out on some beautiful wedding night lingerie in a light eco-friendly hemp-silk mix.

❖ Knicker workshops are a new craze, where you can learn to make your own. Use organic, skin-friendly eco fabrics, and vintage ribbons and lace, to fashion something unique.

❖ Embellish your own favourite underwear with vintage blue ribbons for your 'something old' and 'something blue'.

Corsets

Amazing hand-crafted corsets in modern eco fabrics will help to define your shape on the day. These can be an extravagant purchase, but are tailored to fit and will last for years if well made. Corset-making is a skilled art with a finished piece taking many hours to complete. A design decorated with ribbons and lace will add a feminine touch. You will need to take details of your dress so the corsetiere can work to its shape.

Garters

A frivolous accessory that most brides will only wear on their big day, but a traditional part of any wedding outfit. You can find handmade garters fashioned from salvaged lace and natural silk, and finished with a blue ribbon bow.

Having a Hepburn moment

Gloves can add a chic dimension to any wedding outfit – think of cult screen icon Audrey Hepburn. They come in many lengths, from wrist to above the elbow, in a variety of fabrics to match or contrast with your dress. Pretty lace gloves work well with a delicate dress; heavier fabrics with more structured gowns.

Vintage gloves are usually beautifully made, easily available and often cost only a few pounds from eBay and vintage specialists. Ensure they are scrupulously clean and remember you will need to remove the left-hand glove during the exchange of rings, so make sure you can easily undo any buttons.

Think about dainty knitted fingerless gloves, hand-embellished with tiny beads, for a winter wedding. You could team them with a delicate matching wrap or knitted choker. Gloves can also be useful for early spring or late autumn weddings. If you are wearing a cape, or a bolero or jacket with three-quarter-length sleeves, they will keep your arms warm.

Wedding planner tip:
Always hand-wash silk and hemp silk underwear to keep it looking its best, using a mild, plant-based detergent.

Bags of ideas

It is now perfectly acceptable for a bride (and her bridesmaids) to carry a small bag on the day, sometimes in place of a bouquet. It can hold any items you may need, such as a hanky for those emotional moments or a lipstick for touch-ups. If you are making a speech it's the perfect place to stash your notes.

You will find bags in the most unlikely of places. I was browsing a stall that sold old tools at my favourite outdoor antiques market, and caught a glimpse of something sparkly – it turned out to be an apricot 1930s beaded bag, complete with original vanity mirror. The stallholder told me I could buy it for £5, and I still have it to this day.

You could also ask mothers and grandmothers, or try antique shops and car-boot sales. Charity shops offer thrifty bags, some in as-new condition, from delicate satin clutches to modern patent purses.

Crafting your own

For those brides (or mothers) who are keen to make their own, try the instructions on page 88. This bag is quick and easy to make and you can use pretty fabric remnants you may have at home, or a new eco fabric (see page 64).

Embellish a bag

Even easier is to embellish a bag you already own. Adding a piece of vintage lace, a satin corsage or sparkly brooch can instantly transform a plain bag.

Top bag tips

❉ Enliven a simple dress with a decorative bag.

❉ Gold and silver bags double up as jewellery.

❉ A vintage purse can become your 'something old'.

❉ Decorate with an extra-long ribbon bow for minimal expenditure but maximum impact.

❉ Try a reversible bag for daytime-to-evening contrast.

❉ Be eco-chic and have a go at making your own.

The two bags opposite came from charity shops and were simply embellished with lace and ribbons in minutes.

Wedding planner tip:
If you are having a wedding dress made, ask the seamstress for a little extra fabric to make your own matching bag.

Wedding day bag

This neat bag is the perfect accessory to have with you on the day. It also works well for bridesmaids. This method is great if you come across a garment you love, but which has marks that make it unwearable — and you don't need a sewing machine. I used both the lacy outer fabric and lining of a top I discovered in a charity shop.

YOU WILL NEED:

A4 piece of rough paper

An old top or blouse in a pretty fabric – preferably lined

Piece of plainer fabric if the top is not lined

1m length of 1.5cm-wide ribbon

1.5m length of narrower ribbon in the same colour

Short length of even narrower ribbon

Cotton thread in matching colours

Needle, scissors and pins

An embellishment, such as a button or brooch

METHOD:

1. Place the A4 paper on the garment, with the short side in line with the bottom edge of the fabric, so any pattern runs in the right direction. Pin in place and cut out round it, then repeat with the lining fabric.

2. Fold the outer piece in half, with the right side of the fabric inwards and short edges together at the top. Seam neatly down each side, about 1cm in.

3. Repeat the above two steps for the lining, but leave a gap on one side of about 7cm at the top.

4. On the outer layer, with the right side still inwards, open up the bag and pinch out the bottom two corners. Stitch horizontally across each corner to form equal triangles (see the diagram, opposite). Repeat the above step for the lining material. Turn through the outer layer so the right side now faces outwards.

5. Take a piece of 1.5cm-wide ribbon and pin all the way around the neck of the outer layer, until the ends just touch. Cut the ribbon to this length and unpin. Hem the ends of the ribbon by 5mm.

6. Pin the ribbon back on to the outside of the bag, about 5cm from the top, making sure that the gap in the ribbon is placed centrally. Sew on with 2 rows of stitching, close to each edge, to make a casing.

7. Now, the tricky bit... Place the lining bag inside the outer bag so the good sides are facing each other. Stitch together at the top edge all the way around, about 1cm in.

8. Pull the lining bag up, and pull all of the fabric through the hole in the lining. Sew up the hole, push the lining back down into the outer bag and shake into place.

9. Sew a small, wrist-sized loop of ribbon to the lining, 5cm down from the edge, on the opposite inner side to the gap in the ribbon casing.

10. Cover the loop ends with a vintage button, mini corsage or brooch.

11. Thread the thinner ribbon through the ribbon casing and gather as a drawstring. Tie in a bow and voilà!

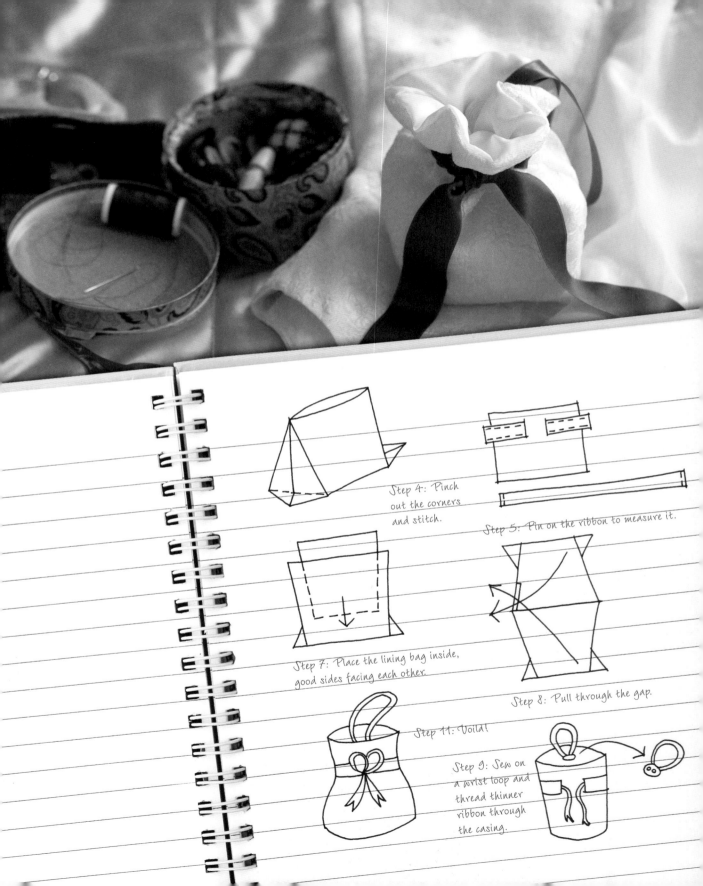

Step 4: Pinch out the corners and stitch.

Step 5: Pin on the ribbon to measure it.

Step 7: Place the lining bag inside, good sides facing each other.

Step 8: Pull through the gap.

Step 11: Voilà!

Step 9: Sew on a wrist loop and thread thinner ribbon through the casing.

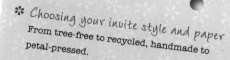

* **Choosing your invite style and paper**
  From tree-free to recycled, handmade to petal-pressed.

* **Wildflower seed paper**
  An easy-to-master method to make your own gorgeous recycled paper.

* **Eco-friendlier printing**
  Old-fashioned letterpress to modern waterless techniques.

* **Making your own**
  Ideas to get you started, and where to learn craft and art skills.

* **E-weddings**
  Virtual invitations and wedding websites.

* **Greener gifts**
  One-of-a-kind presents, charity gift lists and rainforest-friendly guest books.

The Invites

The invitations are the first hint guests will have of your wedding style. I find it helps to let your choice of venue inspire the design: intimate or formal, high glam or laid-back. Eco-friendly invites can be some of the most beautiful you'll find, as old-fashioned art and craft techniques become newly desirable. Letterpress printing, for example, can give you crisp formality, or you could choose a quirky design from an eco-card designer – or learn how to do it yourself.

Alternative papers

*C*hoosing an environmentally friendly paper is a simple way to instantly turn your invites a shade greener. Handmade papers and creatively produced recycled cards will make your wedding stationery distinctive, too.

Recycled paper

This is widely available in a range of colours and finishes. One hundred per cent recycled has a slightly rougher texture than virgin fibre, so for that 'brand new' paper sheen, opt for a blend of recycled content and virgin Forest Stewardship Council (FSC) paper. You can now find pure white recycled paper, too, although you may want to choose an obviously recycled 'fleck' finish as a design statement. The most eco-conscious option is post-consumer recycled, which has already had one use, as a newspaper or magazine. See the Directory on page 208 for details of paper suppliers.

Forest Stewardship Council (FSC)

FSC-certified paper (www.fsc.org) is made from sustainably sourced timber. It is produced using virgin fibre so trees are felled, but new trees are replanted and protected rainforests are never destroyed. When talking to your printer, ask if the paper they are using is FSC accredited, and check for the logo.

Map paper

This is made by cutting old or out-of-date maps into sheets and envelopes. Each piece is unique. Great for a couple who like to travel or who met on holiday.

Decisions about your invites

❊ Would you like your invitation to become a keepsake, or to biodegrade without a trace?

❊ Consider the weight of the paper – heavier invites may be more expensive to post.

❊ Would you like to craft your own stationery, using natural, vintage and reclaimed materials?

❊ Do you want to print your invites on your home printer?

❊ How many invites do you need, and will you want other items of stationery, such as menus, in the same style?

Tree-free papers

These are produced using other naturally occurring fibres, such as coffee and banana skins. Available in either plain sheet form or as ready-made cards you decorate yourself. Some of the papers mentioned below may be made in developing countries. As long as the paper is fairtrade, this is a great way to ethically support a country; however, because of the transport distances, they will have a larger carbon footprint than papers made locally.

ElliePoo

Handmade from elephant dung, this paper carries no odour and is perfectly safe to use. Made using the fibre that passes naturally through the elephant from its wild diet (usually grasses), it is washed a number of times. The resulting paper is cream-coloured with an attractive natural flecking. Another alternative is Rhino Poo paper, while locally made Sheep Poo paper offers fewer 'paper miles' in sheep-rearing nations.

Banana paper

This is made using the waste fibres from banana plantations. By mixing with post-consumer recycled content, the resulting paper is naturally speckled and incredibly strong, with good environmental credentials. Try using it to make paper decorations and flowers (see page 162) as well as invitations.

Handmade

Handmade paper can be plain, or include different natural materials, such as petals, grasses, seeds and leaves. Try coordinating your paper with the table decorations, or even with your flowers. Pink rose petals are gorgeous in paper and can be scattered on wedding party tables to continue the theme.

Seed paper

Perfect for the natural wedding, seed paper can be planted by guests as a reminder of the day. It is available ready-made from companies such as www.elliepoopaper.co.uk and www.zizania.co.nz, or have a go at making it yourself (see my method, over the page).

Recycled and homemade envelopes

You can buy recycled envelopes, but to craft your own take a square piece of paper that fits around your invite and draw faint pencil lines across the diagonals. Take any corner and fold across to one centimetre past where the lines cross. Repeat with the opposite side, then fold and glue the bottom point in place. Fold over the top triangle to form a neat, square envelope.

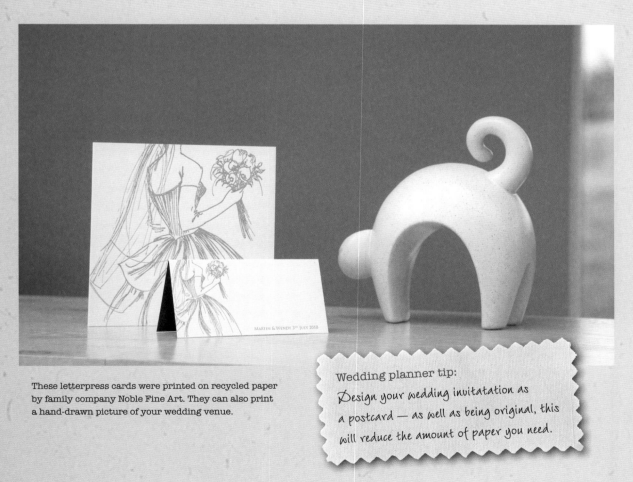

These letterpress cards were printed on recycled paper by family company Noble Fine Art. They can also print a hand-drawn picture of your wedding venue.

Wedding planner tip:
Design your wedding invitatation as a postcard — as well as being original, this will reduce the amount of paper you need.

Wildflower seed paper

The measurements for this recipe depend on how much paper you would like to make. Try it out with a few sheets of scrap paper first, to get a feel for the technique. It can be messy, so you might want to do this outside. I like to add wildflower seeds, but you could also use petals or foliage.

YOU WILL NEED:

At least 2 dry tea towels

A stash of scrap paper offcuts

Deep bowl for blending

Electric hand blender

Mesh tray (available in artist's supply shops)

Large, waterproof, flat container (larger than your mesh tray and at least 10cm deep)

1 packet of small wildflower seeds

1 damp tea towel

METHOD:

1. Lay your clean, dry tea towels to one side of your waterproof container.

2. Shred your scrap paper into small pieces and place in a deep bowl. Cover with water.

3. Using your hand blender, carefully pulse to purée the paper and water into a pulp.

4. Fill your large, waterproof container with water up to about 9cm, and stir in the paper pulp.

5. Scatter in the wildflower seeds, mixing thoroughly (alternatively, you can scatter the seeds over the damp paper in the tray, after step 7).

6. In one quick movement, slide your mesh tray into the pulpy water and lift up, so that you have a fine, even covering of pulp on the mesh. If it is too thick or uneven, plunge the tray back into the water.

7. Scrape the excess water from the underside of the mesh tray with your hand, and place the tray on a dry tea towel, mesh face down.

8. Roll the damp tea towel into a smooth, flat wad and use this to press carefully all over the new paper while it is still in the tray, to squeeze out excess water. Wring out the tea towel between presses.

9. Turn the tray upside down and pat gently to allow the paper to release on to the other dry tea towel. Make sure that the paper is as flat as possible before leaving to dry.

10. Dry for at least 24 hours, then use it to make invites, place names, favour boxes and other stationery.

Wedding planner tip:
If you find your paper is sticking around the edges of the mesh tray when you turn it out, try using the underside of the tray instead.

You can use your paper to cut butterflies to hang from thin thread as decorations.

Follow this diagram to make favour boxes.

Simply fold small pieces in half for plantable place names.

Tie on ribbons to make wishes tags.

Fashionable printing

Whether you prefer the smart, traditional look of letterpress or the rustic individuality of hand-carved wood blocks, there are plenty of printing styles to explore. Eco printing methods have developed rapidly so you don't have to compromise on style or ethics.

Be bold with colour and explore motifs that fit with your theme. A winter wedding I attended had a striking black-and-white colour scheme, and the bride had designed the invitations to match, embellishing them with fine ribbon. The wedding was held at the elegant 18th-century Assembly Rooms in Bath, where Jane Austen would have danced, and the invite decoration was a chandelier in silhouette.

Vegetable-based inks

Using natural vegetable oils, these are much kinder to the environment than regular petroleum-based inks. Many eco printers specialise in veggie inks, and other printers now offer them as an alternative. The colour choice and print quality are just as good as standard inks.

Waterless printing

Conventional printing emits thousands of tonnes of volatile organic compounds (VOCs) into the atmosphere every year and uses vast quantities of water. Waterless offset printing is a revolutionary method that uses no water in its process and has the added benefit of wasting

less paper. The print quality is thought to be better than conventional printing, with a full range of colours. A selection of printers offering this method are listed in the Directory.

Letterpress

This elegant, old-fashioned method of printing is enjoying a revival and lends a touch of old-school glamour to an event. Many letterpress companies still use the original hand-operated antique machines, so their energy consumption is minimal. With an amazing range of typefaces, and the ability to print on to heavy paper stock, it is a fantastic choice for wedding stationery.

DIY

For smaller numbers of invites, using your household printer can be a thrifty option. Larger quantities may use many ink cartridges, which can be expensive, so it may be cheaper to have them printed professionally. Always recycle your empty cartridges – often charities will collect them, or alternatively have them refilled to re-use.

Designer eco stationery

Many companies can both design and print your invites. If you would like to find an artisan craft printer, research local art colleges, check press and local websites for open studios and try US-based crafter website Etsy. Some will design a bespoke invite especially for your big day. Others offer an off-the-peg range of stationery that you can personalise with your own wording. Choose designers using recycled, handmade or tree-free paper, embellished with natural and reclaimed materials.

Always ask for a written quotation listing the items and quantities, and over-order slightly, as you may make mistakes or have last-minute guests.

> Wedding planner tip:
> Order or make some blank place cards in case you want to invite more guests just before the wedding.

Making your own

Hand-crafting your own invitations is fulfilling and can give stunning results. You could design and create a card from scratch, or embellish a plain, ready-made eco card. Collage and simple printing techniques are easy to master, and over the page are some quick-fix decoration tips. Spend a lazy Sunday afternoon playing with ideas to see what works for you both.

Printing stamps and natural prints

This is perhaps the simplest way to craft cards. For a vintage-themed wedding you could invest in some antique wooden printing stamps, like those on page 97. Use letters of varying sizes and typefaces to create a simple but fashionable design.

You can find stamps online, or at flea markets and antique fairs. Keep an eye out for unusual patterns such as lovebirds or flowers.

One of my favourite ways to print natural designs is to use fresh leaves. Choose a leaf with a prominent vein pattern, brush eco paint on to its back and press on to card or paper. Use a single colour with a variety of leaf shapes for a contemporary effect. For more ideas and methods, *Printing by Hand* by Lena Corwin has lots of lovely techniques, including stencilling.

Collage

Cutting, sticking and layering materials can produce a wow-factor card even if you are a relative craft novice. Plan your pattern first, and draw around a template for regular shapes. Use recycled and re-used papers, or magazine pages, vintage fabrics and antique buttons.

Calligraphy

If you are having an intimate wedding, a beautifully handwritten invitation is a delightful indulgence. If you feel your own handwriting isn't up to the task you could ask a friend or find a professional calligrapher.

Tips for home-crafted cards

* Design your invitations so they minimise paper wastage.

* Consider how your embellishments will fare in the post. If you are worried, post a trial invite to yourself to check that it survives.

* If you don't have the skills to make the invites you would love, why not learn them? Workshops are available for techniques such as screen-printing and letterpress.

* Bear in mind the number of cards you will be making, and keep to a process that you feel comfortable repeating.

* Find eco craft supplies online – see the Directory on page 208 for details.

These invites show three easy homemade styles.
Use a hole-punch, and tie with raffia and vintage or re-used ribbon, looping in vintage buttons or other decorations.

Lino cuts

Lino-cutting involves carving a design into a small offcut of lino (supplies are available from art shops, and aren't expensive). You can easily create letters and intricate designs and then print them on to your chosen paper. The block is re-inked between each print, so every card has a charming 'one-off' quality. Check local art colleges for courses, or learn the skills and get expert advice at a craft studio (see the Directory on page 208). If you don't feel artistic, it's easy to trace an existing design on to the lino.

Wood cuts

Wood-cutting is a more skilled method, where you carve the design into a block of wood with chisels. For this you will definitely need to invest some time mastering the techniques, but the finished wood block will make an amazing ornament and memento of your day.

Screen-printing

The ink is squeezed through a stencil on to the paper or card below. You can design and cut stencils yourself or buy them ready-made. It's possible to screen-print on to a variety of media, from handmade paper to vintage textiles. For instructions and inspiration see *Simple Screenprinting* by Annie Stromquist.

Wedding planner tip:
Try framing one of your invitations as a lasting reminder of your special day.

DIY invite inspirations

Decadent ribbons and fabrics, paper butterflies and watercolour paints all add that extra wedding sparkle. Delight in selecting from the range of natural and vintage ornaments at your fingertips. Browse vintage origami books for inspiration – there are some beautiful folded patterns that you can use on cards. Other books I recommend are *Nature Printing* by Laura Donnelly Bethmann and *Good Mail Day: A Primer for Making Eye-Popping Postal Art* by Jennie Hinchcliff and Carolee Gilligan Wheeler; and sample the stationery section at www.allthisismine.com.

Simple embellishments

Ribbons are a fantastic and quick way to give cards a professional finish.

❀ Tie together a paper insert and a card outer using a wide ribbon for elegant simplicity.

❀ Use three strands of thin ribbon in contrasting colours for a candy-stripe theme.

❀ Fashion sumptuous ribbon bows for a decadent look.

❀ Layer heavy vintage ribbon and delicate lace together for perfect winter style.

Quick ways to add your personal touch

Find ready-made tree-free cards and decorate them with natural and reclaimed materials.

❀ Salvage fine wire and shape it into simple patterns such as butterflies or flowers. Fix to the cards using small sewing stitches.

❀ Hand-colour one or two elements of a black-and-white card with watercolour paint or inks.

❀ Print an insert for a bought card on your home printer and assemble the invite by tying with natural raffia.

❀ Gather ribbons around a card and fix in place by threading them through an antique button.

❀ Glue dried petals in a pretty pattern.

Vintage stationery

❀ Search out antique postcards or photo cards. Use as they are (if not already written on) or mount them on to recycled card. Stamp with your chosen text, and embellish with white ribbon and buttons for an individual twist.

❀ Collage an invite using vintage magazines – fashion titles work especially well. Choose a stylish era such as the 1950s – perfect if you will be wearing a 1950s-styled dress.

❀ Cut squares of reclaimed fabrics and mount them on card, then decorate with delicate paper butterflies and brightly coloured ribbons for a summery look.

❀ Trace a 1960s fabric pattern to make your own lino stamp and print this on to handmade paper for a touch of retro style.

Your raw materials

❀ Natural raffia.
❀ Vintage buttons.
❀ Dried flowers.
❀ Lavender stems.
❀ Vintage lace.
❀ Salvaged wire.
❀ Antique beads.
❀ Velvet ribbon.
❀ Shells (sustainably sourced).
❀ Hemp twine.
❀ Organic cotton string.

Wedding planner tip:
Tint the paper, fabric and trimmings for your invites naturally with strong tea or beetroot juice.

We filled this fairtrade card holder with antique cards, mixed with handmade, vintage-style invites by Jessie Chorley.

Escort cards and wedding websites

Not all items on the usual list of additional stationery are necessary, and you may prefer to opt for invites only. Think about combining elements where possible, such as having the wine list on the menu, to keep your 'paper footprint' smaller.

Escort cards

This American tradition has become popular worldwide, and is a novel way for people to find their seats. Guests' names are written on small cards (with the table number on the back or inside) and then showcased in a variety of ways, to fit your theme.

Fairtrade wire card holders come in an array of shapes and sizes. A cream or white heart with scalloped name cards gives a romantic look. The card holder can be hung on a wall or placed in the garden, and re-used after the wedding. Suspend your escort cards from an antique birdcage for a striking display, or use rustic wooden vegetable crates or vintage mirrors to create a fabulous backdrop. For travel enthusiasts, tie named brown paper luggage tags on to an antique leather suitcase.

Thank-you cards

Photo thank-yous are popular and can be prepared by your photographer, or else you can print them at home on recycled card. Alternatively:

* Send all the guests small packets of seeds, wrapped in personalised paper sleeves and tied with vintage ribbon.
* Be kitsch and send each guest a postcard from your honeymoon location, complete with 'Wish You Were Here' motif.
* Save cardboard food or drink boxes from the reception, to craft into pop-art-style cards.
* Keep the petals from your bouquet and use them in handmade paper thank-yous.

E-vites and paperless weddings

E-vites, or virtual invitations, are the greenest option and if you are a whiz on a computer you can create something delightful. Alternatively, there are nifty design companies that will design a fabulous e-vite for you, complete with sumptuous addressed e-envelope. Designs range all the way from minimalist chic to lavish traditional, and you can send thank-yous by email afterwards.

Include a link to your wedding website for guests to RSVP and find event information, such as directions, accommodation and the gift list. With no paper costs or postage to pay, e-vites are a thrifty option. But remember to make a small batch of paper invitations for those guests without internet access or who will treasure an invitation for years to come.

Wedding websites

These are still a fairly new phenomenon but are growing in popularity. You can give web links to local places to stay, ask for guests' special needs, such as dietary requirements, and add fun personalised information such as photos of the bridal party. Think about including a song request page for the DJ or band and a link to your online wedding gift list.

After the wedding, the site can be updated with highlights, photos and thank-you messages, and you can ask guests to upload their own photos from the day. See the Directory for wedding website providers.

Wedding planner tip:
Build your own wedding website and have it hosted by a solar-powered web host for a truly eco online experience.

Greener gift lists

With more people marrying later in life and setting up home before the big day, there is less need for the traditional kettles and ironing boards. Wedding lists today can be for anything and everything, and should reflect your values and style as a couple. If you want to include details with your invitation or e-vite, remember that you will need to decide on the list beforehand.

Eco honeymoon fund

Ask family and friends to contribute to your honeymoon fund, perhaps for two weeks in an eco lodge in Botswana, or five days in a tipi at the Glastonbury music festival. There are some fabulously romantic honeymoon options close to home, from cool camping to eco-chic boutique hotels; for more inspiration see page 192.

Eco-friendly guest books

Guest books capture the memories and sentiments of the day. Look for recycled, FSC-accredited or tree-free papers, and covers made from locally sourced, salvaged wood. Or have a go at embellishing the cover of a plain book with your own pattern of pressed leaves, shell buttons and fine wire. Guests could be asked to sign a special item, such as a photograph, or a piece of handmade paper that can be framed for posterity. One idea I've seen work beautifully is for guests to each bring a leaf, then you have the collection fused in glass to produce a lasting artwork.

A wedding list with a difference.

Ethical stores

Register your wedding list with an online eco store (see the Directory for suggestions). They stock an amazing array of brilliant, energy-saving gadgets, from solar panels to wind-up radios, as well as natural beauty and home wares. Most supply truly fairtrade products, so you can shop safe in the knowledge that your ethics are in good hands.

Other eco presents

❋ Charity lists such as www.oxfamunwrapped.com offer a fantastic selection of 'gifts' that help countries around the world where aid is required.

❋ Or set up a donation website such as www.justgiving.com, to give to a charity close to your heart.

❋ For one-of-a kind gifts, ask your guests to make you something themselves, from jam to cushions, sculptures to renovating furniture.

❋ If you like not-on-the-high-street presents, make a request for 'anything second-hand', from retro childhood board games to a French antique chest.

❋ Perhaps you've always dreamed of owning a patch of native woodland. A wedding fund means your favourite people can contribute to something that you will appreciate for years to come.

Wishes trees

These are charming. Plant a small tree or branching shrub into a decorative pot – perhaps a blossoming fruit tree. Place it somewhere guests will have space to sit and write, and provide a stack of paper luggage tags or cards with ribbon or raffia ties.

Guests note down their message, tie it on to the tree and make a wish. After the wedding, you can collect the tags into a book or special box for safekeeping.

* **Food for all seasons**
  Sourcing your food and choosing a caterer.

* **Produce you can trust**
  Organic and biodynamic, plus foraging tips
  and edible flowers for the adventurous.

* **Home-cooked menus**
  Recipe ideas and growing your own
  fruit and vegetables.

* **Lou's apple and tomato chutney**
  Easy to make from windfall apples.

* **Barbecues, picnics and campfires**
  Ideas for eating outdoors.

* **Drinks for any party**
  From local wines and organic cocktails
  to homemade lemonade.

The Menu

Food to share with friends and family; a meal
to celebrate the beginning of your marriage – that's
the essence of a wedding reception. You can make
it a formal occasion with the best organic, local and
seasonal caterers, or try picnicking in summer
fields, barbecuing on the beach, or hosting
a fashionable tea party. Some of the most enjoyable
meals are those where guests each bring a dish,
so everyone can join in.

Food for all seasons

Planning your menu around seasonal food is the most environmentally friendly choice, as the wedding meal is usually the element of the day with the largest carbon footprint. Often, fruit and vegetables are flown thousands of miles so that we can enjoy them out of season, and most people have lost track of whether products are locally made or grown, or imported.

Try to buy direct from local greengrocers, orchards, dairies and farmers' markets, and ask where the produce comes from. Seasonal foods usually taste better, and are cheaper, too. See our Seasonal Fruit and Vegetables calendar on page 218.

What to ask a caterer

These simple questions will help you judge a caterer's environmental credentials.

❋ Do they source their food locally?

❋ Can they provide an organic, seasonal menu?

❋ Do they use free-range meat, poultry and eggs?

❋ Do they choose Marine Stewardship Council accredited fish?

❋ Do they choose fairtrade products for staples such as sugar, tea and coffee?

❋ Can they compost the food waste and do they buy produce with less packaging?

❋ Do they make their own bread?

Farmers' markets and artisan producers

Farmers' markets are brilliant places to buy directly from local growers and suppliers. Everything from wonderfully flavoured organic vegetables to handmade macaroons, local cream to free-range chicken. Make a beeline for small, artisan makers who take pride in the food they create. The bread on page 116 is from The Thoughtful Bread Company (www.thethoughtfulbreadcompany.co.uk), which uses traditional methods and foraged herbs. Find other artisan producers at www.bigbarn.co.uk, www.organicfoodfestival.co.uk and through our Directory.

Meat and poultry

While organic is the most sustainable farming method, all meat is considered to have a high environmental impact. To reduce your wedding's carbon footprint, why not choose recipes that combine a little free-range meat with a delicious variety of vegetables and other ingredients? This will also be more economical.

Catering choices

Your choice of menu will depend on your wedding style, together with your budget. If your venue is an eco hotel, then you will probably be tied to using its in-house caterers. But if not, specialist caterers can prepare the freshest organic meals, using ethical and local produce. Similarly, you can find dedicated vegan and vegetarian caterers. Look in the Directory for our favourites.

The most expensive option is a three-course, sit-down, plated meal, served at individual tables by waiting staff. If you have a large guest list, or are on a budget, a buffet or tea party will be more manageable.

Finding produce you can trust

*C*hoosing ethical, organic and sustainable produce is good for farm workers, the environment and your health. Whether you are using a caterer or buying your own, free-range poultry, sustainable fish, fairtrade staples and pesticide-free vegetables are all now widely available. For a real hands-on experience, try foraging wild foods.

Organic

Produce labelled as organic is grown without the use of synthetic pesticides, fertilisers, drugs, antibiotics or wormers and is subject to strict criteria set by organisations such as The Soil Association in the UK (www.soilassociation.org). Farmers are encouraged to control pests with natural predators and companion planting, and genetically modified crops are banned. Land that is used to grow food or rear animals must be 'chemical free' for a minimum of two years before organic certification is awarded.

Biodynamic

This established method follows the astronomical calendar to determine when to harvest, plant and cultivate crops. It is based on a self-sufficient farming system, producing natural animal feeds, manures and fertilisers on site. Herbs and special natural preparations (some of which contain animal products) are also used to achieve healthy, strong plants. Demeter (www.demeter.net) is the international certification body.

Fairtrade

Many staple foods are grown in developing countries, where farmers rely on exporting these cash crops to earn a living. Unfortunately, child labour, low wages and dangerous working environments are all too common. The Fairtrade Foundation was set up to stop this (www.fairtrade.org.uk). Look for the international Fairtrade certification mark.

Marine Stewardship Council

The MSC (www.msc.org) promotes sustainable fishing practices and protects the marine environment around the world, and its blue logo guarantees traceability back to a certified source. It helps to ensure that resources are not over-fished, and destructive fishing methods are banned. The MSC can also tell you where to buy certified fish.

Edible flowers
Many varieties can be used in salads and as edible decorations. As with foraging (see opposite), ensure that flowers are picked at their freshest, grown without the use of pesticides, washed thoroughly and used quickly. Research your subject and get to know what is safe to eat. Nasturtiums, calendula, geraniums, elder and rosemary flowers can all be used in recipes and make delectable garnishes.

Slow Food

The Slow Food movement, which began in Italy, is winning worldwide supporters as it says no to fast foods, plastic bags, unethical produce, pesticides and food that has travelled thousands of miles. Instead, it promotes traditional and artisan foods that taste wonderful, and are produced sustainably and ethically, with pride and passion (see www.slowfood.com). Grow your own vegetables, bake bread at home, ask your grandma to write down her favourite recipes for you, and try regional products crafted from ingredients close to home. Slow your pace of life and enjoy food you have taken time to prepare for your wedding feast.

Foraging

Consumers are beginning to realise the foragers' feast available to them on country walks and in their gardens. Some ingredients, such as wild garlic, are easy to spot – just follow your nose. Mushrooms, on the other hand, take a practised eye. Read a good foraging book before you start, to ensure that what you are picking is safe to eat, and never dig up plants. Check out www.wildmanwildfood.co.uk for advice, information, recipes and details of courses, or look at www.wildfoodplants.com and www.eatweeds.co.uk. (My top tip is to avoid picking anything around the base of trees, which may have been popular with dogs.)

> Wedding planner tip:
> Check that caterers can provide sauces and condiments made with free-range and organic ingredients, too.

DIY catering

Preparing your own food is a wonderful way to put your personal stamp on the day and keep your spending down. You can be sure of the origin of your ingredients and lavish lots of care and attention on each dish.

A meal for sharing

Do things a little differently with your catering, and ask family and friends to bring something delicious for you all to share, perhaps suggesting either sweet or savoury, to keep a balance. Non-cooks can bring a bottle of something fizzy instead. If you feel uncomfortable asking, propose this as your wedding gift – much more useful than another toaster. Not only will guests enjoy a wonderful range of flavours, but those with special diets will be able to bring a dish that suits them.

Easy recipes for homemade menus
Wild rice salad ❖ spiced, toasted seeds and nuts ❖ potato salad with baby onions ❖ honey-roast ham ❖ poached fish ❖ home-grown leaf salads brimming with radishes and tomatoes ❖ spinach and wild garlic ❖ char-grilled peppers and mushrooms ❖ homemade bread rolls with tasty herb spreads ❖ free-range mayonnaise.

For winter
Try simple hot foods, such as root vegetable stews ❖ spicy curries ❖ tasty soups ❖ hot flatbreads ❖ bowls of ratatouille.

Follow with simple desserts
Huge pavlovas filled with organic whipped cream and home-grown berries ❖ homemade ice-creams or sorbets.

Big platters

Vintage platters are easy to find in charity shops and markets. Seat guests at long trestle tables, and place your large platters of different dishes down the middle.

Growing your own

If you have a garden or allotment, then it's possible to grow some of your own organic produce for your wedding. There is nothing more satisfying than seeing vegetables spring up from a packet of seeds, or fruit from an unpromising twig in the ground. You can buy organic seeds and plants at nurseries or online. Remember to choose sustainable, peat-free, organic compost so that natural peat bogs are not depleted.

You will need to plan ahead and allow sufficient time to grow the ingredients that you would love to have on your menu. Some, such as broccoli, need many months to mature, while salad leaves can be raised from seed in a couple of weeks. Soft fruit, such as strawberries, raspberries and blueberries, take little effort, and are ideal for summer weddings; serve in meringues or on your cake (see page 124), or use them to make jam.

Windowsill herbs

Herbs such as oregano, coriander and sage are easy to grow, and even if you don't have a garden you can keep them in small pots on your kitchen windowsill. Raise them organically and they will instantly add another dimension to your wedding salads. You could also try fiery chilli plants.

Wedding planner tip:
Serving bowls, platters and large dishes can all be hired if you don't have enough.

My friend Justyn made
gorgeous tarts and salads for
this garden party wedding.

Lou's homemade chutney

Jams and chutneys are some of the most rewarding things you can make with garden or foraged produce. Windfall apples, home-grown onions, damsons and plums can all be easily cooked down and served in small pots with your meal. This is my favourite chutney recipe, which works every time.

MAKES 12 SMALL POTS

INGREDIENTS:

600g windfall apples of any type

2kg red tomatoes

250g red onions

250g white onions

500g unrefined sugar

600ml organic cider vinegar

250g sultanas

1/2 teaspoon dried chilli flakes

1 teaspoon ground cumin

1 teaspoon ground ginger

A good pinch of sea salt

A good pinch of ground black pepper

You will also need a deep-bottomed saucepan or a preserving pan.

METHOD:

1. Peel and chop the onions, tomatoes and apples, and place in a deep pan on a medium heat.

2. Carefully pour in the cider vinegar and stir gently. Add the sugar and sultanas and stir.

3. Mix in the chilli flakes, cumin, ginger, salt and pepper.

4. Simmer for about 2 hours, until the apples are tender and the pan contents have reduced by about a third. During cooking, skim the surface with a wooden spoon to get rid of impurities from the unrefined sugar.

5. Wash your jars and lids in hot, soapy water and place on a clean baking tray, necks up.

6. Put in a pre-heated oven at 180°C/350°F/gas mark 4 for 10 minutes to sterilise. Then remove and cover with a clean tea towel until you are ready to use them.

7. Fill the jars with the chutney and immediately screw on the lids tightly.

8. Allow to cool before labelling the jars with the contents and date. This chutney can be used straight away, but for a more mellow flavour, leave it for a couple of months before eating.

Wedding planner tip:
Peeling the tomatoes first gives a better, more luxurious texture — loosen the skins by covering with boiling water.

As favours, with ribbon ties and luggage tags with guests' names.

You can present your chutney in different ways, depending on your wedding style.

Served simply in mini kilner jars.

With a fabric lid cover and natural raffia bow.

Eating outdoors and perfect tea parties

Checked blankets and pitchers of homemade lemonade, picturesque sunsets and fields full of swaying daisies… picnics make a glorious setting for a wedding reception. They are cheap and fun to organise, too. Look for good-quality vintage wicker picnic hampers in charity shops and markets – full of retro charm and incredibly useful. I found the hamper pictured above in my local charity shop, in perfect condition, for only a few pounds. I customised it by adding vintage crockery and homemade napkins. Often hampers will come complete with place settings for eight.

Ask friends and family to bring along plates of sandwiches or boxes of salads and homemade crisps. And don't forget the bottle opener and glasses.

For big gatherings, rather than transporting large quantities of heavy crockery, you might want to pack some eco-friendly disposables. From plates made out of waste palm leaves (from ethical, sustainable plantations), glasses made from corn starch, cellophane sandwich bags to wooden cutlery, it is easy to source biodegradable options. See the Directory for suppliers.

Barbecues and campfires

Barbecues are fantastic for beach weddings, or why not set one up in your garden for an informal celebration? Look for local, sustainable and fairtrade charcoal; it's now much easier to find. Check with the beach that barbecues are allowed.

A small campfire – on a beach, in woodlands, by a river – is the perfect accompaniment to an outdoor wedding. Use it to make hot drinks as well as meals. Baked potatoes can be cooked in the embers, but need to be checked regularly, and baked apples with sugar and raisins make a mouth-watering autumn dessert.

Above: hand-rolled
jasmine tea. Opposite:
Rocks East – perfect for
woodland receptions.

Hog roast

Mobile hog roasts are available from farmers or caterers
and are always set up outdoors. A whole pig, preferably
organic, is roasted on a traditional spit, and served with
bread and salad. It can feed a large number of hungry
people with ease.

Transporting food

Plan ahead how you will take food to an outdoor
location. Old, wooden vegetable crates lined with clean
tea towels can be used to pack plates and boxes of
food; cover with another tea towel to protect from
insects. When emptied, the crates can be turned over
and used as small tables.

Tea party

Serve dainty sandwiches, home-baked scones with jam
and clotted cream, tiny cakes and pots of hot tea.
In the summer, offer iced tea or fruit cordial instead.
You can make heart-shaped scones with a special
pastry cutter, and serve savoury cheese scones as an
alternative. Try individual cakes decorated with pale pink
icing and shimmering sugared flowers (see page 135),
and handmade fondant fancies in pinks and greens.

Speciality teas

Tea has become fashionable, with all kinds of single
varieties, including connoisseur hand-rolled teas.
Or choose blends of black, green and white tea, or herb
teas. Caffeine-free rooibos (redbush) is rich and mellow.
Always go for organic and fairtrade, and for zero tea
miles, make infusions from the garden.

✤ Spring – fragrant jasmine, delicate Darjeeling, white
   peony tea with rose petals, foraged young nettle.
✤ Summer – cooling peppermint, citrus-scented green
   teas, elderflower, or refreshing fruit infusions.
✤ Autumn – traditional Earl Grey, warming ginger,
   vanilla rooibos, or soothing chamomile.
✤ Winter – smoky Lapsang Souchong, rich Assam,
   frothy chai latte, or spiced cinnamon apple.

Drinks for your celebration

Wines produced by exciting local vineyards will keep down your wine miles; go to a tasting at the vineyard or a nearby supplier so you can try before you buy. The wines on the left come from the award-winning Avonleigh organic vineyard in north Somerset (www.avonleighorganics.co.uk) and Wickham Vineyards in Hampshire (www.wickhamvineyard.com).

High-quality organic wines and champagne-style sparkling wines are now widely available, and biodynamic vineyards produce some of the world's finest bottles. Check labels for low or zero sulphur content if you have dietary sensitivities.

Organic fruit wines have a long history, but are generally not drunk as often as grape wines. Choose from varieties such as elderberry, plum, ginger or tayberry. See the Directory on page 208 for suppliers.

Artisan cider and perry
Specialist ciders and perry (pear cider) are becoming a popular alternative to wine. There are some delicious, light, champagne-method varieties that rival sparkling wines in taste; I particularly like Ashridge from Devon (www.ashridgecider.com). Serve in tall, elegant, stemmed glasses. If you have an orchard and cider press nearby, you could even have a go at making your own cider.

Mulled wine and mulled cider
Rich with the taste of cinnamon, orange and spices, these mixes bring a glow to a winter wedding. Simple to prepare at home, try adding a glug or two of brandy before serving for extra warmth.

Homemade cordials and lemonade
Fragrant elderflower cordial and zesty lemonade are superb non-alcoholic alternatives that are easy and cost-effective to make yourself. Buy organic, unwaxed lemons and scrub thoroughly before use. Pick your elderflowers from traffic-free spots, and wash thoroughly. Use fairtrade, unrefined sugar and store in recycled bottles. In the winter, offer guests your own mulled elderberry cordial made from dried elderberries and spices – delicious and great to keep colds at bay.

Mineral water
Ideally, serve tap water in pretty glass jugs, to reduce water miles and waste. If you do opt for bottled, choose a nearby supplier who sources from a local spring, and buy in large containers. Recycle bottles and see if you can buy on sale or return. FRANK water (www.frankwater. com) sends all profits to developing countries to help them improve their own water supplies.

Organic cocktails

Bramley & Gage (www.bramleyandgage. co.uk) produces delicious liqueurs from home-grown soft fruit using traditional French methods. For an elegant, summery drink, mix sparkling wine or water with raspberry liqueur and serve with a raspberry in the bottom of the glass. Delicious.

HEDGEROW SLING

50ml organic sloe gin

25ml fresh lemon juice

12.5ml Bramley & Gage blackberry liqueur

Soda water, or naturally sparkling water

Shake the sloe gin and lemon juice with ice and strain over fresh ice into a Collins glass. Top with soda and float the blackberry liqueur. Garnish with fresh blackberries and a lemon slice.

❋ How to choose your perfect cake
Those all-important colour schemes.

❋ Baking a wedding cake
Tiered, stacked and extraordinary.

❋ Contemporary cupcakes
From jewel colours to classic white,
and a fail-safe recipe.

❋ Tarts and meringues
Cakes that are out of the standard mould.

❋ Decorate your own
Using flowers and foliage, heirloom
jewellery and vintage ribbons.

❋ Frosted petals and chocolate curls
How to make your own simple
edible decorations.

❋ Imaginative displays
Vintage cake plates and stylish stands.

The Cake

The wedding cake has to be the most delicious
element of the day. You can really have fun with it,
regardless of how formal the wedding. There are all
kinds of exciting possibilities, from brightly coloured
cupcakes to classic elegance, or a modern sculpture
in chocolate. Some of the prettiest cakes I've seen
have been iced plainly, then decorated with soft-
petalled roses, or each tier topped with close-packed
raspberries. The only limit is your imagination.

Choosing your perfect cake

Everyone loves a wedding cake, and you can find styles to suit the most unusual of celebrations. Some sit happily as part of an afternoon tea at a relaxed summer garden party, while others can take centre stage in the grandest country house. You can be greener with your cake by choosing local, seasonal and ethically sourced ingredients, and save pennies by having the cake double as your favours or dessert.

Your cake personality

Your choices of venue, dress and flowers can help you find your cake 'personality'. Look for inspirations in your wedding day notebook (see page 32) and books such as *Cakes for Romantic Occasions* by May Clee-Cadman, which is lovely, and *Cake Chic* by Peggy Porschen. The www.thecaketress.ca website has some amazing designs, too. Save offcuts of dress fabrics and ribbon to help when selecting decorations.

At one outdoor wedding, with playful ribbons in the trees and the groom arriving in a decorated camper van, the bride chose a birdcage cake by The Utterly Sexy Café (www.utterlysexycafe.co.uk), iced in pastel blue with ornamental garlands of magenta icing flowers. But if your own dream wedding is more formal and Grace Kelly in style, with floor-length gown and hundreds of guests, an elegant and traditional white, tiered cake, with fresh white roses, is gorgeous.

Colours and decorations

Cakes can be created in any colour imaginable, from bright turquoise to shocking pink. You could even have each tier in a different colour. With combinations of icing, ribbons and flowers it is easy to match your cake to your wedding colour scheme.

For a dramatic look, team a base of black icing with delicate, white, filigree piped icing (see page 125). This is easy to do at home yet gives a professional result.

If you are not keen on icing, simply stack light sponge cakes. Add a generous dusting of icing sugar and decorate with plump seasonal berries.

Baking your own cake can be an enjoyable challenge and help your budget, too. You may be surprised at what you or your family can achieve. Alternatives such as tarts and mousse cakes can be served as part of a meal.

Remember that your cake needs to feed all your guests, so calculate quantities carefully. Bear in mind the time of year you are getting married, as the availability of seasonal ingredients will vary.

Professional cake bakers

An online search or asking locally will turn up a host of cake bakers. Prices and ethics vary, so shop around and always check references. Book a tasting session before you order, to try different types of cake and icing, and don't be afraid to ask it they use organic and local ingredients. To reduce your food miles, try to choose a baker who is closer to the venue; some venues will even bake the cake on site.

If you would like to do the decorating yourself, many bakers will provide a plain iced cake: this keeps costs down and you can exercise your artistic flair. Alternatively, you can have a homemade cake professionally iced and decorated: ideal if you love your mum's fruit cake but don't want her to worry about her icing skills.

Your ingredients

Maybe you can barter with neighbours for fresh eggs, or make your own fruit preserves. Local magazines and web guides will lead you to nearby farms, mills and farmers' markets. See the Directory for websites listing producers in your area. By taking time to choose your ingredients carefully, you will rest easy knowing your cake does not have a large carbon footprint or contain synthetic additives – and it will taste great.

Rachel at Planet Cake (www.planet-cake.com) uses eggs from her own hens. She crafted the flowers from sugar paste, so it's all edible.

Wedding planner tip:
Cover plain cake boards with a layer of white icing to give your display a professional finish.

Baking your own cake

Making your own wedding cake needn't be daunting. It means you know exactly what it contains, and you can choose your own favourite recipe. Plan ahead and have a trial run if possible, especially for the decorations. Take photographs of the finished cake, make an equipment and ingredients list, and time the whole procedure. By estimating how long it will take to decorate your final cake, you can calculate when it needs to be baked.

Fruit cakes can be kept in an airtight container for weeks but a sponge only has a shelf life of a few days. If you are planning on keeping a top tier for a christening, always choose fruit cake, as it will freeze easily. For recipes, *Delia's Complete Cookery Course* is my must-have bible, and for information, courses and equipment try Squires Kitchen (www.squires-shop.com). You can make your own decorations (see page 132) or buy them ready made; with either it's possible to create beautiful designs with minimal effort. The Planet Cake (www.planet-cake.com) buttercream stack on page 120 shows how simple you can go. Dip strawberries in slightly cooled, melted dark chocolate, leave to set on greaseproof paper, then zigzag with melted white chocolate using a piping bag.

Mum's finest

Family members and close friends will be thrilled to be involved and might even make the cake their wedding gift to you. Have a chat beforehand and show them photos and sketches so they understand the cake you are envisioning. Hiring the baking tins or stands and buying ingredients will help them out. Remember transportation on the day of the wedding: check if they are happy to deliver the cake to the venue, and provide sturdy boxes or an extra pair of hands if required.

Which style of cake?

Tiered cakes

This formal design usually has three or more tiers of different sizes, suspended above one another on pillars. Always ask for white plaster or timber pillars and timber dowels to keep things natural. Unless you are experienced with tiered cakes, my advice is to leave this style to the professionals. An easy way to create an elegant tiered effect without the worry is to use a tiered cake stand. You can hire these and then simply place a cake, on its board, on each level.

American stacked

A more modern style – most of the tiered cakes shown in this chapter are stacked. Here, the tiers are placed directly one upon the other. When kept simple, this can be a beautiful option, and can be decorated with elegant trimmings such as ribbons and vintage jewellery. You still need dowels and boards, but the home cook can easily achieve a two-tier stacked cake.

Contemporary designs

Many bakers now offer extraordinary contemporary cake designs, from striking sculpted chocolate to edible rice paper creations. Whether you dream of a breathtaking long and low ice-white winter scene or a tall tower of dark chocolate curls, the only limit is your budget.

If baking your own, search in specialist shops for unusual cake tin shapes, and see page 135 for instructions on making chocolate curls.

Maya made her own wedding cake. Here she is showing filigree icing, using her own design. The dots make it an easy technique to master.

Versatile cupcakes

These colourful cakes have become extremely popular. They can be served as a cake course or pudding, or even used as favours. Recipes range from traditional sponge to mini fruit cakes, gluten free to spiced carrot. All can be baked and decorated by the most inexperienced of home cooks, and there will be a flavour to suit all your guests, regardless of taste or dietary preference. For display ideas see page 136.

Vintage
Decorate the edge of the paper case with lace and ribbons, neatly secured with a small dot of icing. Serve on floral vintage crockery with miniature antique cake forks.

Traditional
Use pure white icing and select only white decorations, such as small sugar flowers or delicate dots of filigree icing. Try icing and decorating the cakes in three different styles and then mixing them up. White cakes on a tiered cake stand can give the impression of a traditional, tiered cake.

Contemporary
Choose bright shades of icing, or even glossy dark chocolate, and combine with fresh flowers in vibrant shades for dramatic effect. On a tiered cupcake stand, try placing a fresh flower between each cake. Arrange the blooms just before serving so that they don't wilt, and check that they are safe to be in contact with food.

Natural
Match vanilla icing with unbleached paper cases and sugared petals made from edible garden flowers that are in season (see page 135). Decorate the stand with raffia for a naturally beautiful display.

Delicious cupcake tips

❊ Use muffin tins and muffin cases, and fill only halfway up. This means you will have room for piped icing.

❊ Why not gather your bridesmaids and friends for an evening of baking. Make sure to bake a few extras to 'test'!

❊ Pipe butter icing on to the tops – a star-shaped nozzle is best. Ice from the edge of the paper case inwards.

❊ Alternatively, 'flat ice' the cakes with a small palette knife dipped in hot water.

❊ You could also pipe on whipped cream and decorate with fresh seasonal fruit – but prepare these cakes at the last minute and be sure to refrigerate them.

Top: elegant white from www.countrycupcakes.com. Above: sugar flowers are easy to find and quick to apply.

Lou's gluten-free lemon cupcakes

You can find all sorts of options for regular sponge cakes — the classic formula is to weigh three eggs and use the same amount of flour, butter and sugar. Below I've given you my favourite gluten-free recipe, as these can be more difficult to track down. This recipe can also be baked in one large tin.

MAKES 12

INGREDIENTS:

Paper muffin cases

175g unsalted butter

175g golden caster sugar

2 beaten eggs

125g ground almonds

Finely grated rind and juice of 1 unwaxed lemon

50g gluten-free plain flour

½ teaspoon gluten-free baking powder

75g polenta flour

METHOD:

1. Preheat your oven to 180°C/350°F/gas mark 4.
2. Line a muffin tin with greaseproof muffin cases in a colour of your choice (remember they are going to be on display).
3. Beat the butter and sugar together until pale and creamy, then stir in the eggs and almonds, and the lemon rind and juice.
4. Sift the gluten-free flour and baking powder on to this mixture, add the polenta flour and stir gently until combined.
5. Carefully spoon the mixture into the paper cases, being careful not to spill any on the sides. Only fill the muffin cases halfway (to allow room for the icing).
6. Bake for 20 minutes or until they are firm to touch. If in doubt, gently test with a skewer: if it comes out clean, they are done. (The cakes will have risen but will still be below the paper case line.)
7. Transfer to a wire rack and allow to cool completely.

Use a star-shaped piping
nozzle — it's quick and easy.

Group on a vintage cake
stand for a tea party.

Show them off
in individual
sundae dishes.

Create a traditional cake
effect by stacking on
a tiered cake stand.

Alternative cakes

Of course, you don't have to serve cake at all – this is an opportunity to be original. Many of these alternatives can be made by home cooks, although some do require skill. If you would like your tiered wedding cake to double up as dessert, choose a sponge recipe and serve with homemade fruit coulis or local ice cream.

The cheese cake

Wheels of your favourite local cheeses can be stacked as you would a traditional cake, and decorated with fresh flowers or fruits – ideal if you don't have a sweet tooth. Cut in the usual way and serve to your guests after the meal with homemade crackers and seasonal fruit. (Bear in mind that blue and soft cheeses can have a distinctive scent, and are not recommended for pregnant women.)

Fruit tartlets

Tiny mouthfuls of buttery pastry, delicious patisserie cream and fresh fruit are delightful and easily made at home. They can be displayed as you would cupcakes (see page 136); include a slightly larger tart for the bride and groom to cut and share.

Mini meringues

These are light and sculptural, and a perfect thrifty choice. Topped with fresh cream and berries or sugared edible flowers, they can also be your dessert.

Little mousse cakes

These perfectly formed stacks of vanilla sponge, whipped cream and fresh fruit or chocolate mousse can be assembled with a small, removable patisserie ring (found in cookware shops and online). Dust with icing sugar and top with chocolate leaves or marzipan fruits for a light and delicious cake substitute, and serve with tea on dainty china. Vary the mousse flavourings to give different colours, such as strawberry pink or blueberry lilac.

Sweet individual cheesecakes

These can look completely at home at a wedding if they are carefully baked and decorated. Mixing dark and white chocolate in your fillings gives a contemporary marbled effect. If serving as a pudding, add a fruit coulis to cut through the richness and add a touch of elegance.

Mini wedding cakes

These are literally mini versions of a full-size cake, with perfectly smooth icing and sumptuous decorations (see the photograph on page 137). They look elegant stacked on a tall stand and are ideal as favours – but you're best asking a local cake specialist to make them for you.

A note about chocolate

Cocoa beans come to us from countires with a favourable growing climate, such as Venezuela, so they will always have a larger carbon footprint than local produce. But there are plenty of organic and ethical brands; ideally, check for fairtrade accreditation marks.

If you are feeling adventurous you could try making your own raw chocolate – it's surprisingly easy. You'll find courses, instructions and cocoa beans to order online (see www.chocolatealchemy.com and www.williescacao.com). The results are delicious, and you can make it sugar-free, too. Plain raw chocolate is also stocked in health-food shops.

Decorations for your wedding style

From velvety roses to delicate gypsophila, glossy holly to sunny prairie blooms, fresh flowers and foliage will give your cake a seasonal, natural charm. There are also many inventive vintage and homemade possibilities. Non-edible decorations will need to be removed before the cake is sliced, so let your caterer know that you want to save them as a memento.

Flowers and fruit

Make the most of seasonal blooms. The cake on the opposite page has been dressed with flowers that can easily be found in the late spring: early roses, and white lilac and bluebells from a friend's garden. If you are on a budget, you could choose a small posy for your bouquet and transfer it to the top of the cake after the ceremony. Some flowers, such as nasturtiums, are edible, but make sure that any flowers you use have been grown without pesticides.

Colourful fruit can turn a plain cake into a culinary masterpiece. Heap seasonal ripe berries on to each tier of a stacked cake and dust with icing sugar for a mouth-watering, professional display.

Raffia

One of the natural products I like best, raffia can be used to great effect on cakes of all types. For simple country chic, take about twenty long strands and tie in a big bow around the waist of a white iced cake.

Vintage jewellery

If you are wearing vintage jewellery with your wedding outfit, you could incorporate a matching brooch into the design of your cake. Marcasite and anything sparkly works well, particularly antique dress clips and buckles. Tie a long satin ribbon around the top tier of your cake and fix your find to the centre of the bow for instant glamour.

Ribbons and trims

Search online shops such as www.ragrescue.co.uk and www.nearseanaturals.com, and visit vintage fairs (see the Directory) for all manner of trimmings, from ribbons and tassels to Christmas bells. A large, blousy antique silk flower looks fabulous on the top tier of a cake, teamed with vintage ribbons in a matching colour. Or make your own sugar paste ribbons and bows, as seen on the cake pictured left (see page 134 for how to do it).

Tea lights

These are stunning for a late evening wedding. Place the tea lights in small, clear glass holders, sit them on the top tier of a royal iced cake, and surround with small fresh flowers. Be sure to choose unscented, plant-wax candles, and check that other decorations are not flammable.

Paper flowers

If you love trying new crafts, have a go at making beautiful paper flowers for your cake (see the paper flower pomander on page 163). There are courses and many books on the subject that include patterns. You could even fold origami flowers from edible rice paper.

A beginner's guide to icing types

Royal icing

Traditional, hard sugar icing, usually bright white.
Fairly easy to make and use if you have a steady
hand and the right equipment, but it sets like rock.
Royal icing can only be used with fruit cakes, and
they must be covered with marzipan first.

Sugar paste (regal ice)

A soft, roll-out icing. Popular and easier to use than
royal icing, it gives a rounded edge to the cake
tiers. You can decorate the cake by crimping:
making small, decorative pinches with a tool found
in sugar-craft supplies shops.

Pastillage

Absolutely beautiful. An advanced technique that
uses sugar dough formed into intricate sculptures.
I would advise you to go on a course if you want
to learn the skills.

Butter icing

Delicious, and easy to whip up. Usually used for
small cakes or large sponge cakes, and can
give a sharp edge to the tiers. The UK version is
ivory-coloured and has a short shelf life due to the
butter content. US buttercream often uses white
vegetable shortening for a purer white icing.

Recognise this cake? It's the same basic,
butter-iced stack as on page 120. Rachel from
Planet Cake has made a space with two cake
boards for florist Tallulah Rose to fill with flowers.

Sugar paste, glitter and chocolate curls

Edible decorations are ideal for a natural wedding – at the end of the big day whatever is not eaten will biodegrade. It is easy to make your own, but if you are not sure of your sugar-craft skills you can also buy ready-made sugar flowers and decorations.

Edible cake toppers

Sugar paste figurines of the happy couple are available ready-made in a range of styles to match your theme, or you could have a go at making your own. You can also buy sugar flowers of many kinds: the roses on this page came from a local shop.

Glitter you can eat

Edible glitter is a relatively new concept in cake decorating but is proving popular as a dusting for cupcakes and to give a sparkle when added to the icing of larger cakes. You can find glitter made from natural gum arabic, as well as from sugar.

How to make sugar paste bows

A simple yet extremely elegant way to decorate a plain cake with the minimum of fuss. Tint some sugar paste icing to match your wedding accent colour and roll out to about 5mm thick.

Cut long, straight ribbon strips of matching width (25mm works well) and secure them around the bottom of your cake tiers with a little sieved apricot jam. Make a bow using the same width strips and allow to dry and harden before fixing to the cake. Cut the ends of the bows into little V-shapes for a professional finish. These work particularly well on square tiered cakes.

Edible decoration ideas

* Giant chocolate buttons – choose organic fairtrade in white, milk or dark.

* Seasonal fresh fruit.

* Chocolate shapes and leaves – make your own or buy from www.montezumas.co.uk, who are very ethical, or www.traidcraft.co.uk for fairtrade.

* Sugared edible flowers.

* Rice paper flowers – easy to make (or buy) and highly effective.

* Sugar paste ribbons and bows.

* Edible glitter.

Make your own chocolate curls

YOU WILL NEED:

Fairtrade organic chocolate (dark should be 70 per cent cocoa solids)

A cold, hard surface, such as a granite worktop or a chilled baking sheet

A sharp knife and flexible palette knife

Greaseproof paper for the finished curls

METHOD:

1. Melt the chocolate slowly in a bain marie (or in a bowl over a pan of just-simmering water), stirring gently with a wooden spoon.

2. Take off the heat and spread the chocolate on to the cold surface in a thin layer using the palette knife. Allow to cool.

3. Once cooled and solid – but not rock hard – use a sharp knife or cheese shaver to scrape up into individual curls. Place on greaseproof paper to set in a cool place or in the fridge for a couple of hours.

Make your own edible sugared petals

YOU WILL NEED:

Greaseproof paper

Caster sugar

1 egg white and a few drops of water

Three handfuls of fresh edible flower petals, washed and patted dry

Small artist's paintbrush

Wedding planner tip:
For a professional touch, marble the chocolate for decorations such as leaves or curls by partially mixing white and dark.

METHOD:

1. Put a sheet of greaseproof paper on a baking tray and dust with caster sugar.

2. Lightly whisk the egg white and water in bowl until just frothing, then paint the mixture on to the petals in a thin layer. Hold the bottom tip of the petal carefully in your fingers or with a pair of tweezers. Be careful to cover the whole petal surface with egg white, or your flowers will go brown.

3. Dust the petals with caster sugar and place on the greaseproof paper. Repeat, then allow to dry out completely in a warm, dry place. They keep for a few days in a dry, airtight container, but go soggy in the fridge.

Showing off your cake

Wedding cakes can make a wonderful centrepiece for your celebration. Elaborate icing deserves to be fully appreciated, so try placing your cake in front of a vintage mirror to allow your guests to see all angles. For a relaxed outdoor reception, you can achieve a more rustic look by sitting your cake on a tree stump or upturned antique vegetable crate. Make sure that it is level and out of the way of inquisitive children and pets.

If you are having a small wedding with one long trestle table of friends and relatives, position the cake in the middle as a focal point, and surround it with flowers, foliage and candles. This works particularly well for winter and Christmas-themed weddings, and means the cake will be centre stage in photos.

Imaginative touches

Flowers, foliage, clean driftwood and shells, leaves, petals and fruit will all create beautiful and unusual displays around the base of your cake. Save magazine pictures and look at www.devondriftwooddesigns.com for inspiration. Ivy cascading down the length of a table makes for a magical effect.

Any individual cake can be presented as a favour for a guest, whether it's a cupcake, tartlet, mini meringue or pastry. If the cake is delicate, or you are worried about flying insects, place it in a clear cellophane bag and tie with a ribbon or raffia. Cellophane is made from plant cellulose and is fully biodegradable.

For unusual and theatrical table settings, serve cupcakes in vintage teacups, or group perfect mini cakes on vintage shelves, or in an apothecary's chest.

I always enjoy hunting around flea markets and antique centres, and collecting Victorian tiered wire and wrought-iron plant stands. These work beautifully as alternative cake stands. Clean thoroughly and revive with a coat or two of natural paint; afterwards, you can re-use the stand for your plants.

Displaying cupcakes

❀ Show them on vintage glass cake stands or plates gathered from charity shops or flea markets – keep an eye out for rare coloured glass. Group the stands together in threes for a stylish effect.

❀ Hire a professional tiered cupcake stand. These are available in anything from three tiers to eight. You can decorate the edge of each level with a thin ribbon in a complementary colour.

❀ Use a Wilton stand. This is a professional wire stand that holds each individual cupcake at a slight angle, like branches on a tree. Good if you are only having a small number of cakes, but make sure the stand you order is for the correct number.

❀ Be bold and line your cakes up along a narrow table. Interweave them with flowers, petals, leaves, ivy and raffia.

❀ Place a small flag or sail in each cake with the name of the guest. Alternatively, have the names iced directly on to the cakes as edible place markers.

❀ Serve in pretty 1950s glass sundae dishes as a thrifty dessert.

❀ Add interest with gorgeous cupcake wrappers. Available in recycled paper in pretty and intricate designs, such as butterflies, you wrap them around the plain case to add a professional finish. Try making your own from real petal paper for a thrifty cake upgrade; find templates and instructions online. You can scallop the edges with shaped craft scissors.

Rachel made several variations of these
Planet Cake blossom mini cakes, and
we displayed them in a set of vintage
champagne saucers.

Wedding planner tip:
Square wedding cakes are much easier to
cut and serve neatly than circular cakes,
and they look elegant, too.

❋ *Flowers through the seasons*
Local and organic flowers, working with
a florist and DIY workshops.

❋ *Growing your own blooms*
From delicate wildflowers to elegant lilies.

❋ *The perfect bouquet*
Styles for all dress shapes, and how to tie
your own gorgeous bouquet.

❋ *Wellington boots to vintage vases*
Unusual and inventive ways to dress your
wedding with flowers.

❋ *Herbs, pots and leaves*
Delicious table herbs and decorative
ideas for foliage.

❋ *Nature's confetti*
What could be more natural than petals?
Presenting your confetti with style.

The Flowers

Local and seasonal flowers, and cottage garden
and prairie blooms, are in vogue – and not just at
green weddings. The beauty of seasonal flowers
is that the variety and colour palette change
throughout the year. I love the seasonality of flowers,
and choosing a species associated with a particular
time – early spring anemones, or midsummer
poppies – means that bloom will always remind
you of your wedding date.

Seasonal blooms

Seasonal flowers are the best choice for a natural wedding, especially when grown locally. There are gorgeous natural options in every season – take a look at the Seasonal Flowers calendar on page 219 for inspiration. The hellebores used as a hair decoration on page 183 bloom from late winter, while evergreen foliage and fruits can be used to make stunning displays.

Themes throughout the year

* Spring – early-flowering bulb plants in unusual pots, such as brightly coloured hyacinths.
* Summer – vintage vases filled with roses, peonies and sweetpeas.
* Autumn – big bunches of golden sunflowers, or late-season rich colours and seedheads.
* Winter – festive wreaths with rosehips, crab apples, fir cones and cinnamon sticks, or hand-crafted paper flowers (see page 163).

Most shop-bought cut flowers travel hundreds, if not thousands, of miles by air or sea, creating an enormous carbon footprint. Instead, buy local flowers from farmers' markets and smaller, cottage garden growers. We have used www.bathorganicblooms.co.uk, www.sweetlovingflowers.co.uk and www.countryroses.co.uk. Seasonal blooms are less expensive and often fresher, too.

Organic, fairtrade and biodynamic flowers

Look for flowers certified by organisations such as The Soil Association or UDSA, or grown biodynamically under the Demeter mark, which have not been sprayed with pesticides. If you have your heart set on a flower that isn't in season at the time of your wedding, try buying fairtrade blooms. There are many other eco and ethical certification systems worldwide, so check for their marks (see page 219, and page 110 for more information).

Floral workshops

Why not create your own wedding flowers? Once you know the basics, you can easily make arrangements, buttonholes and posies. Floristry workshops are a great place to find out tricks of the trade, the equipment required and which flowers complement one another. My friend and talented florist Rachel, from Tallulah Rose Flower School (www.tallulahroseflowers.com), taught me how to make the hand-tied bouquet on page 146.

Jane Packer's *Flower Course* is a brilliant book full of hints and tips, and among Paula Pryke's titles I particularly recommend *Seasonal Wreaths and Bouquets*.

Planning with a florist

You may wish to employ a professional florist, especially for a large celebration. Good florists are worth their weight in gold and can create breathtaking arrangements to suit your wedding style and budget. Choose one who can provide you with seasonal flowers, preferably from a local source, and follow up references. Flowers can be one of the most expensive wedding services, so ensure that you have a budget in mind before you meet. And take along a picture of your wedding gown and proposed hair style to help them design your bouquet.

Wedding flowers

* Bridal bouquet.
* Bridesmaids' bouquets and men's buttonholes.
* Flower girl posy or willow wand.
* Church arrangements.
* Pew ends or chair decorations.
* Table centrepieces and mantelpiece displays.
* Door wreaths and hanging pomanders.

Jo Illsley of Bath Organic
Blooms grew the flowers
for her own wedding.

Growing and sourcing flowers

Even if you are a novice gardener, it is relatively easy to grow your own flowers to cut and arrange in vases, or raise plants and herbs to display in their pots. You can glean ideas from open gardens and plant nurseries, and borrow books such as Sarah Raven's *The Cutting Garden*. If you are planning your wedding a year ahead, see what is in bloom in the month you are marrying. Friends may have established plants already in their gardens, or be happy to plant some for you. Join an organic gardening charity such as Garden Organic for advice (www.gardenorganic.org.uk).

If you are lucky enough to have an allotment, or good-sized kitchen garden, set aside one bed for your wedding flowers in the run-up to the big day. Saving seeds, or joining a local seed swap, where you swap spare seeds with like-minded people, are thrifty options.

Wildflowers

Although it is tempting, never pick wildflowers while out on country walks – take photographs instead. Wildflowers, such as cow parsley, are of enormous benefit to local wildlife and support natural ecosystems. If you would like to display wildflowers at your celebration, grow your own at home for harvesting in time for the big day. Seeds are available from garden centres or online sources such as www.organiccatalog.com and can be grown with little effort. Or buy them from cottage garden growers.

Wildflowers are extremely delicate and can wilt shortly after cutting. So grow them in unusual pots and containers and display the flowers as growing plants.

Farmers' markets

These are wonderful places to buy local flowers direct from the growers. Imagine galvanised buckets full of wide-open anemones or bunches of vibrant cornflowers tied with raffia. Take a camera and ask questions about the flowers' origin and longevity. Many growers will be able

to take orders for collection the day before the wedding. When buying local, seasonal flowers bear in mind that weather conditions may affect what is available.

Cottage garden flowers

In colours from pure white through sugar pinks and pale lilacs, on to deep purples, I love fragrant sweetpeas. Try using a single colour for an elegant but informal bridal bouquet. Cut the stems quite short and tie with wide satin ribbons for a professional finish.

Dried flowers and wheatsheaves

Naturally dried wheatsheaves, barley-sheaves, poppy heads and teasels can be bunched together as you would a hand-tied bouquet and secured with raffia or ribbon as a centrepiece. For a more elaborate display, mix in fresh blooms such as roses or lavender. A mini version makes a lovely, country-style bridal posy.

Wedding planner tip:
Calla lilies are easy to grow at home and make a striking bridal bouquet, suitable for the most glamorous of weddings.

Your bouquet style

The shape and colour of your bridal bouquet or posy will be guided by your dress. Have you chosen a formal gown, which will be best complemented by an elegant bouquet filled with structured flowers and foliage? Usually these bouquets feature a single colour theme. Or will you be wearing a cocktail, prom-style or flowing empire-line dress, which will be enhanced by gentle, delicate posies? For these styles, you could try wildflowers or cottage garden blooms in a mix of colours, loosely tied together.

Bouquets for dress styles

❋ Formal – hand-tied bouquets.

❋ Prom-style – spherical posies or pomanders.

❋ Empire line – single flower stems.

More petite brides benefit from teardrop-shaped bouquets to lengthen their frame, while taller brides can carry off spherical arrangements with ease.

Don't forget that bouquets, like dresses, can be embellished to match your theme. You could include vintage lace (which has been used to wrap the sweet william bouquet to the left), antique brooches or an heirloom silk flower.

Bridesmaids

Usually bridesmaids will carry a smaller version of the bridal bouquet. As an alternative, think about pomanders, corsages or posies, and keep to the same colour scheme but vary your choice of flowers.

Flower girls

Small posies or pomanders, or even decorated willow twig wands, make perfect floral accessories for children. Make sure that they are reasonably robust, as they will inevitably be thrown around with exuberance on the day.

Buttonholes for the seasonal groom

Buttonholes can add a special touch to a groom's outfit. Traditionally, buttonholes are worn on the left, and the groom has a more elaborate design than his best man, ushers and groomsmen.

Herbs make fabulous buttonholes, whether teamed with a flower head or on their own. Rosemary signifies remembrance, so if there are family or friends who cannot be there, this is a nice way to remember them. Avoid using large, open blooms as these can

become damaged over the course of the day; compact, smaller flowers, such as roses, are classically elegant.

Failsafe fixing

Florists often supply buttonholes and corsages with magnetic fixings. In my experience, often these are not robust enough and do not work on more flimsy fabrics. Instead, ask for large-headed pins, which you can weave through the fabric and over the stem. If in doubt about how to do this, ask your florist to fix the buttonholes and corsages on the morning of the wedding, or show the best man so he can take on the task.

Wedding planner tip:
Fragrant, white-belled stems of lily-of-the-valley make an elegant yet fresh bouquet for all dress styles.

Bouquet tips

❖ To help wild or cottage garden flowers last, plunge the bottoms of the freshly cut stems into boiling or hot water, then put straight into a vase.

❖ Take bouquets out of water half an hour before needed and pat the stems dry on a clean tea towel to avoid drips and water marks.

❖ Cover unsightly stems with wide, satin ribbons for an elegant finish.

❖ If arranging your own bouquet, remember to remove thorns and anything that could catch on your dress.

❖ Remove lily stamens, which can stain fabrics and skin.

Hand-tied wedding bouquet

This easy technique was taught to me by Rachel at Jallulah Rose Flower School. You can use whatever flowers are in season, in your preferred colour scheme, and match the ribbon to a flower or your dress.

YOU WILL NEED:

Your selection of flowers

Foliage stems that complement them

Twine

Florist's shears, or other tough scissors or secateurs

1m of 2cm-wide ribbon or vintage lace

A pin

1m of 2.5cm-wide ribbon or vintage lace

Fabric scissors

METHOD:

1. Condition your flowers by removing lower leaves, thorns and stamens (which can stain clothing).

2. Separate your flowers and foliage into types and lay each bunch in a group on your table.

3. Take the first flower – the largest type – and cross a second bloom over the top of the first in your hand (as shown in the second photograph, above).

4. Select a different flower and cross it over the other two stems.

5. Twist the bouquet and add another flower or piece of foliage. Repeat until you have used each different type of flower. Remember to keep twisting your bouquet in the same direction, and to check the shape from every angle. Look in a mirror to help you judge if you are forming the flowers into a pleasing arrangement.

6. Continue twisting and crossing stems until you have a tight, rounded bunch with a 'twisted' stem shape.

7. Tie the stems securely with twine, then trim the stems with the shears so they are all the same length.

8. Wind the narrower ribbon neatly around the stems so that it covers at least 3cm. Secure with a pin.

9. Wrap the wider ribbon around and tie into a bow at the front, making sure the pinhead is covered. Trim the ends into pretty V-shapes with the fabric scissors.

10. Keep your bouquet in water until needed, but be careful not to submerge the ribbon.

Wedding planner tip:
I have used a number of different flower and foliage shapes, but kept it coordinated by choosing only whites and greens.

Step 4: Add a third flower, crossing the stems.

Step 5: As you cross more stems they make a twisting pattern.

Step 7: Cut the stems all to the same length.

Your finished bouquet.

Individual displays

Any container can be a potential vase. Vintage bottles, antique vegetable crates, goldfish bowls, rustic galvanised buckets, glass sundae dishes, enamel jugs, glass test tubes (with a single bloom in each), or wire mannequins – all will add personality to your displays. Most types of flower container can be hired from your florist, or buy your own in flea markets, charity shops and online.

Cut-glass and ceramic vintage vases

These are wonderful for brightly coloured, blousy, country-style blooms. Old varieties of roses, gypsophila, peonies and tulips look fabulous simply bunched into vintage vases. Ideal for a garden party wedding: team with single flowerheads displayed in vintage teacups, and teapots brimming with flowers.

Contemporary

For a simple and effective display, float flower heads and delicate plant wax candles in a bowl of water. Thrifty yet stylish, this technique also works well for small ponds (use a fishing net to retrieve the candles).

Alternatively, hang single flower blooms on fine cotton thread at differing heights from beams, window frames, tree branches or a string 'line'. Choose robust flowers such as roses and leave 1cm of the stem to tie the cotton on to. This can be stunning in buildings with delicate structures, such as orangeries.

For another elegant, modern look, line up mismatched old glass bottles and place a single bloom in each.

Hay bales

If you are using hay or straw bales for informal outdoor seating, try sinking a sturdy vase or bucket into the bale so the lip of the container is flush with its top. Half-fill the vase with water and arrange your flowers. Place vases at the corners of the bale for maximum impact.

Wellington boots

Clean wellington boots make a humorous and charming display. Although waterproof, the boots can be unstable when filled with water. To steady them, fill the bottoms with heavy stones first. Choose cottage-garden colours, arrange the flowers in a loose style and pair the wellies on your tables. If you love this idea but are not keen on having boots on tables, stand them in doorways and in corners to catch guests' eyes.

Jam jars

For an outdoor wedding, a wonderful way to denote an 'aisle' is to use recycled jam jars filled with flowers hung on to wooden stakes or poles. To create a hook for the jar, tie floristry or recycled wire around the neck and twist into a hook or handle. Short-stemmed sweetpeas, cornflowers and peonies look amazing displayed in this way. For a fairy woodland theme, use mini jars and single blooms, and hang on willow branches.

Herbs, pots and foliage

One of the most eco-friendly ways to incorporate flowers into your celebration is by using potted plants and herbs. This allows them to go on living after the wedding and leaves no waste. Give to guests as a lasting keepsake at the end of the day.

Herbs as flowers and to eat

Herbs are some of my favourite wedding flowers, as they are so incredibly versatile. Sweet-scented herbs, such as lavender and rosemary, make gorgeous displays, while others, such as thyme and basil, can be eaten as part of the meal: encourage guests to pick the fresh leaves to accompany their food. (A zingy, home-grown tomato tart is enhanced by a few tender basil leaves, while rock hyssop is delicious on risottos.)

For table centres, you could plant herbs in antique terracotta pots and tie with vintage ribbons, or choose herbs that come in natural coir pots, such as those from The Hairy Pot Plant Company (www.hairypotplants.co.uk). Decorate these biodegradable containers with natural raffia for a fully plantable decoration. You can also buy your own natural coir pots online from eco garden suppliers: choose mini pots for small herb varieties, or large ones for centrepieces. Try unusual containers, too, such as food tins with the labels removed, or vintage teapots.

Branches and blossom

All year round, you will find interesting foliage in the garden, both evergreen and deciduous. If you are marrying in the spring, take advantage of the abundant blossom on trees and bushes, from bright yellow forsythia to pale pink cherry.

Bare winter twigs and branches pruned from garden trees can be decorated with lanterns, or with fresh flowers hung in mini jars, for a fashionable room display. Boughs of catkins, soft leaf buds or tiny blossoms look fabulous in tall enamel jugs or old milk churns.

Unusual pot plantings

From brightly coloured daisies to tall, waving sunflowers, mini rose bushes to deep purple hyacinths, you can present growing flowers in interesting pots and containers.

❋ Group pots of small plants in odd numbers on tables. For a modern feel, use pots of the same size and line up in rows; for a country look, use different sizes and group more loosely.

❋ For an outdoor wedding, plant small flower varieties in vintage wooden seed trays. Place on the centres of tables and decorate with matching ribbons.

❋ Use vintage ceramic vases as pots and plant with wildflowers to bloom in time for your wedding.

❋ Daffodils, hyacinths and snowdrops make an uplifting springtime display. Plant them into unusual containers, such as vintage tins and wooden bowls.

Evergreen ivy

Whatever the time of year, ivy can be found scrambling up walls and covering the ground, and it is easy to cultivate at home. Team with large blooms, such as roses, for an elegant look, or with wildflowers for a more rustic feel. One couple on a tight budget were holding their reception on a narrowboat. I draped the cabin with muslin and ivy bunches, transforming it from a plain, utilitarian interior into a mini wedding marquee.

Wind ivy around staircases and along tea-light-dotted mantelpieces for a winter theme, or use it as the base for a wreath with pine cones and cinnamon sticks. (Check beforehand that you are not allergic to ivy.)

Petal confetti and giving flowers away

Biodegradable confetti is the only choice for a natural wedding. Don't be tempted to ask the guests to throw rice after the ceremony: wild birds tend to eat it and it then swells in their stomachs. Instead choose natural petal confetti, either fresh or dried. It can be found in every colour imaginable, to match any wedding theme. Some dried petal confetti will stain if it becomes wet, so if you are worried about rain, choose white petals to avoid accidents.

Dried petal confetti

As dried petals are much lighter than fresh, they take longer to fall through the air, giving more opportunity to catch that confetti photograph. The beautiful confetti opposite came from Shropshire Petals (www.shropshirepetals.com); I would also recommend www.petalpot.co.uk. Here is a guide to the different colours available:

* Pinks – roses, peonies, hydrangeas, heather.
* Blues – hydrangeas, delphiniums.
* Yellows – sunflowers, roses, jasmine.
* Oranges – marigolds, roses.
* Whites – delphiniums, roses, hydrangeas.
* Lilacs – hydrangeas, lavender.
* Reds – roses, hydrangeas.
* Greens – hydrangeas, roses.

Fresh petals

The best flowers for fresh confetti are roses of any type – even the small, tight ones – as they have lots of petals. About twelve roses should be enough for a large basketful. You could ask local flower stalls for blooms past their best at the end of the day, which would otherwise be disposed of. Florists can also provide fresh petal confetti, as they may have flowers that are not good enough quality for displays, but are fine for confetti.

How to make fresh confetti

* Take two bunches of garden, local or fairtrade roses.
* Wrap your hand around the whole flower head.
* Pull gently, in a twisting motion.
* The petals should come off in one bunch, leaving behind the centre part of the bloom.
* Gently separate the petals into a bowl, basket or paper cones.

Displaying and distributing your confetti

To minimise paper wastage, place your petals in one big glass bowl or basket, and ask guests to help themselves. Or give your flower girl a pretty basket of confetti that she can hand out to guests as they leave the ceremony. For an outdoor wedding, she could scatter petals down the 'aisle'.

Alternatively, you could make your own confetti cones out of recycled or handmade petal paper and arrange them in a basket, box or bowl. A nice touch is to make the cones from seed paper containing the seeds of your confetti flowers (see page 94). Guests can then take home the cones and plant their own confetti.

After the big day

You may have decided to give all your flower displays to guests, but if not, you could ask one of your bridesmaids to take them to a local retirement home. Displays will often last for a good week after the wedding. Floral arrangements made for churches and chapels may be left at the venue for other congregations to enjoy; check that the church is happy for you to do this. Table confetti, cake flowers and displays that have been out of water for some time should be composted, but remember to re-use any trimmings, such as ribbons.

❋ *Going natural with decorations*
From fruits and driftwood to pebbles, plus seasonal style tips.

❋ *Something different*
Sky lanterns, ribbons and bicycles.

❋ *Vintage details*
How to theme your wedding with crockery, antiques and fabrics.

❋ *Handmade and homemade*
Gorgeous paper flowers to natural soaps.

❋ *Teacup candles*
Find out how to make eco-chic lighting.

❋ *Decorations on a shoestring*
Plus ethical buys and thrifty raw materials.

❋ *Favours to make at home*
Delicious truffles and scented lavender bags.

Decorations

Choosing a seasonal or vintage theme will make your decorations eye-catching without costing a fortune. Search out the best green suppliers and products hand-crafted by artisans, or have a go at making your own. Decorating your wedding with flair, whether a simple ceremony or a lavish celebration, will wow your guests and give your day its own unique atmosphere. And it is simpler than you might think to achieve a beautiful, natural wedding setting.

Natural decorations

Fruits, flowers and foliage can all be used to style a wedding day (for more about flower displays, see page 148). Collect and beachcomb driftwood, pebbles, leaves and twigs. By using objects from nature, sourced locally, you can be sure that your trimmings will have a minimal carbon footprint and will biodegrade or can be returned to their environment.

Ways with fruits, flowers and foliage

* Fruit – use as place names by tying a miniature luggage tag on to the stem. Guests can eat the fruit as part of the meal.
* Driftwood – place clean, pale driftwood down the centre of a long table and intersperse with plant-wax tea lights.
* Leaves – scatter russet or golden dried leaves on the tables, or wrap fresh leaves around candles.
* Blossom – gather blossoms and scatter on tables and in gardens.
* Pebbles – use as place markers: either paint on the name of the guest, or tie on a small tag with rustic twine.

Beach weddings

Let your imagination fly with what is naturally available. Build sandcastles with intricately moulded buckets and jewel them with collected shells; they could outline an 'aisle' or standing area. Draw patterns in the sand, gather pebbles to make heart shapes, and tie reclaimed fabric on to willow twigs to make gently swaying flags or windmills. Group together flowers in tin cans with beachcombed driftwood.

Seasonal ideas

* Spring – dainty wildflowers, spring bulbs and pots of grasses and herbs. Choose from sweet-scented jasmine, exotic-looking hellebores, magnificent magnolia blossom and fresh, green foliage.
* Summer – bunting in the trees, antique galvanised watering cans bursting with local flowers and strawberry plants in pots for guests to help themselves.
* Autumn – rich, red leaves and glossy berries, deep-coloured blooms and willow twigs, teasels and other dried seedheads, pumpkins, decorative squashes and rosy apples.
* Winter – plant-wax candles, log fires, storm lanterns, holly, winter white flowers, natural ivy, fir cones, cinnamon sticks and rich, sumptuous ribbons.

Trees and herb favours

Tiny trees in plantable coir pots make fabulous favours that will last a lifetime. Choose a native species or try raising your own baby saplings from acorns and collected seeds. Baby herb plants are wonderful gifts, too; grow them in small, antique terracotta pots, or present the plants in a hessian bag. To make the bag, cut a square of natural hessian four times the width of the root ball, pop the herb roots into the centre, and gather up the corners. Tie a piece of string, ribbon or twine around the neck and fasten in a bow. See *Jekka's Complete Herb Book* and www.jekkasherbfarm.com for varieties and advice.

Home-grown snowdrops in coir pots are teamed with Jessie Chorley's handmade table numbers.

Wedding planner tip:
Recycle Christmas decorations for a festive theme — place delicate glass baubles in tall, clear vases for a striking centrepiece.

Original and unusual

Stage a wonderful display with antique planters, old jam jars and even bicycles – see if salvaged and recycled bits and pieces can be given a new lease of life. We created the wedding notice on the left with two flea-market-bought French wire plant-holders, and a handmade wooden sign, painted with natural paints.

For the garden party wedding that you see throughout the book, I covered wooden trestle tables with plain white tablecloths, then laid beautiful vintage and charity shop lace cloths over the top. Cut-glass vases and jugs, collected over the years, were filled with country-style flowers, from blousy pink peonies to fragrant white stocks. In between these I arranged old glass and silver candlesticks holding plant-wax candles.

The places were set with mismatched vintage crockery, and the look was completed by my homemade napkins, in different fabrics, tied with offcuts of ribbon. The result is something you could create yourself – or else add your own original elements and personality.

Sky lanterns

Drifting skywards on a summer evening, sky lanterns are a magical, romantic decoration. Made from paper, with a beeswax disc that you light to send them into the air, they are silent and completely biodegradable. They are much more environmentally friendly than fireworks, which will scare wildlife. Visit www.skylanterns.com, who deliver worldwide.

Ribbons in trees

For a seaside wedding I hung the branches of the surrounding trees with vintage and recycled ribbons and pretty glass lanterns. It worked for both daytime and evening. So quick and easy to put up, ribbons are a cost-effective decoration and look fabulous if cut long so they can catch the breeze. Choose colours to complement your theme.

Bicycles

If your style of dress allows it, arrive at your wedding on a bike, with veil flying, for an amazing photo opportunity. Embellish your cycle to make it the perfect wedding transportation.

❖ Baskets – fill the front basket with armfuls of seasonal blooms.

❖ Pannier – secure the bridal bouquet on to the rear pannier.

❖ Signs – direct guests to the reception with your bike: hang a sign from the crossbar and decorate with flowers and foliage.

Handmade wooden signs

If you need signs for your event, why not make your own from timber? Salvage wood – preferably planks with the bark still on the edges – and use a soldering iron to 'write' on to the surface for a rustic effect. You could also use large printing stamps with waterproof inks or paints.

Mirrors

Prop antique or vintage mirrors from charity shops and online auctions behind displays of flowers to create an illusion of depth. Or lay them flat and arrange pillar candles on top to reflect the light and, more practically, catch any wax drips. You can always change the colour of frames by repainting them.

Wedding planner tip:
Place jam jar lanterns next to marquee tent pegs to help guests avoid tripping over the guy ropes at night.

Vintage themes

From 1970s flower power to 1950s chic to delicate Victorian – vintage elements can fit both traditional and alternative weddings. If you are not sure where to start, find a vintage object you adore, such as a teacup or candlestick, and build your decoration style around that.

Crockery

I love vintage – and especially crockery. Everything from tea sets to cake stands, glassware to milk jugs. I started collecting years ago and now have a huge blanket box filled with my finds, which I hire out to couples for their wedding or party – you can see a few of them pictured opposite and on page 171.

For your own, look in junk shops, at car-boot sales and in charity shops to kit out your wedding for minimal cost. Don't forget you can always sell on crockery afterwards. Once friends and family know you are collecting for your big day, you will probably be showered with their collections to borrow or keep. Mix and match designs for a deliciously eclectic look, and place vintage teacup candles (see page 164) on shelves and tables, and in gardens. See the Directory for vintage hire companies.

Ornaments

Antique and vintage ornaments can all be used to great effect on tables, mantelpieces and outdoors. Glass candlesticks, pretty ceramic birds, candelabras and strings of beads are an easy way to theme your day. Pick them up at charity shops and flea markets for a small outlay and donate them back to charity afterwards.

Jewel favours

For female guests, buy small vintage brooches and pin on to their napkins. This does not have to be expensive but will create both a lasting favour and a fabulous decoration.

Bunting for all occasions

Bunting is ideal for weddings, silently dancing in the breeze, tied on to trees or around marquees. Debbie Coutts (www.tatteredandtorn.co.uk) made the gorgeous bunting on page 154. She uses only reclaimed and vintage fabrics and trimmings, tints them with tea and plant dyes, and sews the flags by hand. Try making your own, perhaps in different shapes, such as hearts or stars and embellish with vintage buttons and ribbons.

Retro details
* 1950s teacups in single colours.
* 1960s brightly coloured art glass vases.
* 1970s floral tablecloths.
* Victorian glass candlesticks.
* Antique lace.
* Vintage teacup candles (see page 164).
* Salvaged vintage newspapers.
* Retro magazines.

Delightful place names

�֍ Try vintage playing cards, traditional postcards or antique photo cards. Write the name by hand in large letters in a contrasting colour.

�֍ Salvage retro magazines and cut out quirky adverts or pictures to paste on to recycled cards.

✲ Secure vintage newspapers (sepia tones work well) on to recycled paper as a backing for a hand-printed name.

Handmade and DIY

Embellish your wedding with delightful decorations skilfully handmade by local artisans, or have a go at making your own with natural, recycled and biodegradable materials.

Paper and fabric flowers

Gorgeous and available in a rainbow of colours, these can be arranged in the same way as fresh flowers. Look for handmade paper blooms, or choose fabric blossoms sewn with vintage materials; a bouquet fashioned from salvaged lace and silks can be just as beautiful as a fresh posy and will last a lifetime.

The paper roses opposite were created by skilled maker Wendy Morray-Jones, who bases her designs on a vintage pattern book and cuts each petal individually. Search on craft site www.etsy.com for techniques and inspiration.

Recycled sculptures

Artists and designers can craft unusual decorations out of reclaimed wire, wood and metal, from tiny birds to delicate snowflakes. Some of my favourites are from www.rookywood.org.uk. Group them together as a centrepiece, or arrange on individual place settings.

Glass hanging ornaments

These catch the light beautifully and are usually handmade from recycled glass. Tie on to willow branches or hang from trees for an outdoor celebration. Look at www.henandhammock or www.southernrata. co.nz for handmade and recycled ornaments.

Wooden name tags

Great for decorations and also guest favours. Buy tags with a small hole in one end so you can thread them with a ribbon and tie on to napkins or favours. Or else make your own tags by salvaging offcuts of reclaimed wood and printing words or names on to them with old printing blocks.

Table plans

If you are opting for a traditional large, written table plan, try displaying it on a timber easel decorated with seasonal blooms and foliage for a secret garden feel. Enclose it in a gilt picture frame so you won't need to mount it on card. Outside a marquee, use a blackboard on an easel for guests to write messages, or to chalk up the menu.

For a striking display, suspend place cards from an antique birdcage. Alternatively, old rustic wooden vegetable crates or pretty vintage mirrors create a fabulous backdrop. Travel enthusiasts will appreciate named brown paper luggage tags hung in an antique leather suitcase, and for an outdoor wedding, simply tie them on to tree branches with natural raffia.

Soaps

Natural soaps make fantastic decorations and favour gifts. Either buy them from a local natural skincare company or have a go at making your own – look for soap-making workshops online or at the craft spaces in the Directory on page 208. Choose small soaps decorated with dried rosebuds or lavender, wrap in brown wrapping paper and tie with ribbons and twine. Add a recycled paper name tag and place on napkins for a gift and place name in one.

Wedding planner tip:
If you are making your own soaps, bear in mind that they will take about six weeks to 'cure' and be safe to use.

Paper roses by Wendy
(www.wendymakesroses.com)
formed into a pomander by
Rachel of Tallulah Rose Flower School.

Teacup candles

Simple to make yet incredibly effective. Find your plant waxes and natural wicks from reputable suppliers to ensure that they are clean-burning and eco-friendly, and buy teacups from charity shops. After the wedding, clean the cups and either make more candles or use them for tea again.

YOU WILL NEED:

Tiny elastic bands

Wooden cocktail sticks

A selection of pretty teacups and saucers

Natural wax, such as soy or rapeseed

Double-boiler pan, or a heat-proof bowl and saucepan it can sit in

Natural wicks with metal sustainers attached

Wooden spoon

Scissors

METHOD:

1. Hold two cocktail sticks together and secure each end with the elastic bands. Repeat until you have the same number of these as cups.

2. Heat the teacups by placing them in a warm oven for 5 minutes.

3. Melt a spoonful of the wax in the double boiler, or heat-proof bowl, over simmering water. Gently dab on to the bottom of the metal wick sustainer.

4. Quickly position the sustainer in the bottom of a cup, in the centre. (If you prefer, you can use glue dots instead of the wax.)

5. Place the cocktail stick 'wick holders' across each cup, threading the wick between the sticks until secure and upright.

6. Pour the wax into the double boiler and heat until it melts and reaches the temperature recommended on the packet. Stir at all times and be careful not to overheat.

7. Carefully pour the melted wax into each teacup, making sure that the wick holder does not move. Fill to 1cm below the top of the cup.

8. Leave the cups until completely set – do not move or knock them during this time.

9. Trim the wicks to 5mm long with sharp scissors.

10. Arrange at your wedding and enjoy.

Wedding planner tip:
Try mixing a little beeswax into your wax blend to give the candles a wonderful, honey scent.

Step 5: Thread the wick up between the sticks of the wick holder.

Step 7: Pour the melted wax up to 1cm from the top of the teacup.

Step 9: Once fully set, trim the wick to 5mm in length.

Decorations on a shoestring

For those on a tight budget, simply beg, borrow and make everything you need. Freecycle is a great resource for finding items for free – after the wedding, recycle them back into the system or give to charity (www.freecycle.org). Or why not borrow eye-catching decorations from friends and family?

My money-saving tips include using timber picnic tables so you don't need tablecloths, and making your own bunting from pretty, charity shop bed sheets. Cut the sheets into rough triangles of the same size, and stitch on to 'ribbon' from the same fabric. Candy stripes or florals give different looks, or else mix them up. Don't worry about frayed edges – they are part of the charm. Arranging your own flowers is also good for the budget: garden varieties such as hydrangeas in simple, contemporary glass can look stunning. And for the ultimate fuss-free reception, host a picnic or barbecue – which needs little adornment other than the bride and groom, some friends and food to share.

Glass bottles
Re-use wine bottles to hold dinner candles or hand-dipped tapered candles, or to display single-stemmed flowers. Keep the labels on if they are interesting; soak with black tea to make them appear aged. Fill wide-necked bottles with bunches of flowers, either fresh or paper. Decorate with ribbons, strings of charity shop beads, or raffia tied into a big bow. Raffia is inexpensive, and can be used to decorate everything from chairs to candlesticks.

Pots, jars and tins
Large, clear glass pots or jars filled with fir cones, fruit, pebbles, leaves or sand can make an interesting base for either candles or flower displays. Some items can quite happily be immersed in water but others, such as fir cones, are best left dry.

Fill other containers with small plants or sweets. Flowers look charming arranged in tins or jam jars, and remember that the smaller the jar or vase, and the narrower its neck, the fewer flowers you will need – which can also help to keep costs down.

Hiring
Hiring is often a more affordable alternative to buying. You can even find smaller finishing touches, such as butterfly decorations and table numbers (see the Directory).

Fairtrade decorations
If you need to buy anything from further afield, look for products bearing the Fairtrade logo, from paper flowers to hand-printed fabrics, festive baubles to storm lanterns. Search online ethical stores or fairtrade shops and find our favourites in the Directory.

Cheap and gorgeous

Raw materials
❀ Vintage buttons.
❀ Homemade wildflower paper.
❀ Bunting made from scraps of fabric.
❀ Charity shop tablecloths.
❀ Recycled ribbons.
❀ Big bunches of natural raffia.

Pots and jars
❀ Vintage terracotta.
❀ Coir pots.
❀ Tin cans.
❀ Glass jam jars.
❀ Wooden bowls.
❀ Vintage cocktail glasses.
❀ Sundae dishes.
❀ Wide-necked bottles.

Fairtrade ideas
❀ Wire card holders.
❀ Tea-light holders.
❀ Hand-printed napkins.
❀ Strings of paper flowers.
❀ Hand-sculpted ornaments.
❀ Plant-wax candles.
❀ Handmade paper cards.

Creative lighting

Lighting is important as it helps to establish a special atmosphere. Candlelight and lanterns are both warm and flattering, and create a romantic ambience perfect for weddings.

Jam jars and hand-blown lanterns

Jam jar lanterns are a thrifty yet pretty adornment. Collect jam or chutney jars in the run-up to your wedding and wrap a salvaged wire around the neck. Bend a hoop of wire over the top and either leave as they are or decorate with a ribbon. They look magical hung from trees or on beaches.

Hand-blown fine recycled glass lanterns can be used to decorate tables and line pathways. Try filling them with water and using as vases for a pretty hanging flower display.

Tin can candles

Following the candle method on page 164, half-fill an old food tin with plant wax and leave to cool completely. To create a lantern effect, punch a few holes in the sides of the tin, above the level of the candle, using a bradle and small hammer. Add a wire hook if needed.

Pumpkin lanterns

For a memorable and quirky seasonal decoration, carve pumpkins into intricate butterfly or flower pattern lanterns and place in the centres of tables, or in hidden corners indoors or outside.

Vintage candlesticks

From Victorian glass to antique silver, candlesticks can dress any table or display. Collect together clear glass candlesticks in different sizes and arrange them in groups of odd numbers, such as threes or fives, in the centres of tables. Or try alternating short and tall candlesticks between vases of flowers. Use dinner candles made from plant-based waxes fragranced with essential oils, but be careful not to place candlesticks near open windows or drafts, as the breeze will make the candles drip and burn more quickly.

Candelabras

Stylish and graceful, candelabras always suit formal weddings. Either decorate with flowers, as shown opposite, or leave unadorned and light cream, plant-wax candles for elegant simplicity. Look for antique or vintage candelabras, perhaps borrowed from friends, or rent from a good hire company.

Eco-friendly candles

Regular candles are petroleum based and usually have synthetic fragrances. They can give off smoke and toxic chemicals as they burn. Instead, choose clean-burning candles made entirely from plant wax. Candles that are naturally fragranced with pure essential oils smell wonderful and can have therapeutic benefits, too.

Beeswax candles

Long-burning beeswax candles smell divine. They are available as either poured container candles or hand rolled from sheets; try to buy those made from organic beeswax, and look out for kits containing everything you need to create your own rolled dinner candles. (Remember that beeswax is not a vegan product.)

Tea lights

Plant-wax tea lights are delightful, creamy little candles. They tend to burn for considerably longer than regular tea lights and are often made from soy wax. Soya is a cash crop and sometimes protected rainforest is destroyed in order to plant it. So look for candles made from sustainably farmed soy, produced without such deforestation, from the likes of www.hapibean.co.uk.

A feast of homemade favours

Favours are traditionally given as a thank-you token to guests for attending your wedding. From heavenly chocolates to personalised cards, you can make all manner of gifts that will please your friends, young and old. Think of unusual options that say something about you as a couple. I recently attended a wedding in Wales where they gave mini packets of Welsh cakes (a traditional type of fruit drop scone).

Truffles

Decadent little rounds of soft chocolate, dusted with fine, fairtrade cocoa powder, melt-in-the-mouth truffles are simple to make at home. Prepare them just a few days beforehand, and keep them cool.

Homemade sugared almonds

Serving five sugared almonds is the original favour gift to symbolise wealth, happiness, health, long life and fertility. But rather than buying preservative-laden shop varieties, try cooking your own caramel-scented sweets with fairtrade organic almonds.

Heart biscuits

Delicious butter biscuits are a cost-effective treat. Use a heart-shaped cutter and pack the cookies into biodegradable cellophane bags, tied with a natural raffia bow. For extra decoration, add coloured icing and a dusting of edible sparkle. For a Christmas wedding, choose a holly or tree cutter and pierce a hole at the top of the biscuit before baking. Once cooled, thread with a ribbon so they double as tree decorations.

Favour boxes

Tiny decorative boxes are extremely popular to hold gifts, from trinkets to flower bulbs. Mass-produced boxes may have travelled many miles, so make your own, or buy boxes made from recycled or handmade paper and those bearing the Fairtrade mark.

The most eco-friendly favour boxes are plantable ones made from wildflower seed paper (see page 94), which can grow in guests' gardens after the wedding. Look online for templates, and opt for a design in one piece, like the box above, rather than with a separate lid. They require less paper and are easier to make.

Seeds

Wrap organic seed packets in paper sleeves, hand-printed with details of your wedding. For a surprise, decant seed packets into handmade paper envelopes, decorate with a vintage card and tie with a plush ribbon (remembering to include growing instructions).

Lavender bags

Gorgeous scented lavender bags are easy to sew and thrifty. For each bag, cut two heart shapes from a reclaimed fabric, preferably with a small pattern. With right sides outwards, fill the centre with dried organic lavender flowers and top-stitch neatly by machine or hand all the way around, 1.5cm in from the edge. Carefully trim the edges with pinking shears and finish with a ribbon loop, fixed in place with a vintage button.

Paper scrolls

Combine name cards and favours by writing the table name or number, together with a personal message, on a small piece of handmade paper and rolling into a scroll. Display in alphabetical groups in terracotta plant pots or glass vases.

❄ *Skincare for everyone*
What makes truly natural brands special.

❄ *A naturally healthy glow*
My guide to eco cosmetics, and how
to keep blemishes at bay.

❄ *DIY pampering*
Decadent home spa treatments to keep
the whole bridal party stress free.

❄ *Face masks good enough to eat*
Try strawberries, avocado and oatmeal.

❄ *Gorgeous hair*
DIY hairstyling and tips from
the professionals.

❄ *Finishing touches*
Natural fake tans, and ways to stay relaxed
and fresh faced on your big day.

Natural Beauty

The best beauty preparation for a bride-to-be is a good
skincare regime and plenty of relaxation. I've been
using and learning about natural products for many
years now, and am delighted whenever I can pass
on what I've discovered to my friends and brides.
As well as delicious skincare brands and secrets,
I've included some simple relaxation techniques and
pampering treats. Enjoy them as you get ready for
your big day and as part of your future lifestyle.

Ingredients to avoid

Parabens, mineral oils, synthetics, sulphates, SLS, silicones, nano particles, GMOs, phthalates, carbomers, DEAs, artificial colours and animal-tested ingredients. See the Glossary on page 217.

Organic skincare

Natural and organic skincare is increasingly popular, and a regime based on plant products will contain fewer manmade chemicals, a number of which can trigger allergies. From the simplest range for sensitive skin, to cutting-edge, plant-based brands, there is a solution for all brides (and grooms). If you are changing from a synthetic product, give your skin a few weeks to adjust. You may get some blemishes at first, but drink lots of water and persevere – your skin will thank you for it.

Creams made from vegetable, fruit and nut oils, nut butters and beeswax, fragranced only with pure essential oils, are good for the planet as well as your skin. You can find out more, including skincare recipes, from *The Green Beauty Bible* by Sarah Stacey and Josephine Fairley, and *Natural Health and Body Care* and *Recipes for Natural Beauty*, both from Neal's Yard Remedies.

Why choose non-synthetic?

The skin is the largest organ of the human body and a significant percentage of what you apply is absorbed into your bloodstream. Most standard skincare products contain chemicals that are either synthetic or petroleum based, and studies have shown that a number of these ingredients can have a detrimental effect on skin health.

Some mainstream companies have realised that consumers are examining labels more closely and have removed parabens and SLS (sodium lauryl sulphate, a harsh de-greasing detergent). Nonetheless, labelling can be deceptive: some products marked 'natural' or 'plant-based' only contain a small proportion of ingredients derived from nature. The way to tell if a cream or lotion is really natural is by checking the ingredients list and looking for logos such as The Soil Association, BDIH, Ecocert, OFC and USDA. A few products in our Directory may contain tiny amounts of food-grade preservatives, but have been included because of their otherwise outstanding environmental credentials.

Your natural essentials

Cleansers
Cream or oil-based cleansers are great for dry skin, especially those with sesame or jojoba oil. Coconut-derived rinse-off cleansers suit normal to combination skin.

Toners
Try rose for sensitive skin, neroli for dry and lavender for problematic skin. Atomisers that you spray on will minimise cotton wool waste.

Serums and elixirs
These advanced anti-ageing products, designed to plump fine lines and add radiance, use beneficial plant extracts that firm and tighten skin. Apply sparingly under moisturiser.

Facial oils
A great alternative to day or night cream, these pure botanical oils leave skin nourished, not greasy.

Moisturisers
Fragranced only with essential oils, these protect against atmospheric pollution as well as hydrating the skin. Neroli and shea butter are good for dry skin and rose for dehydrated; frankincense has amazing anti-ageing effects.

Face masks
Apply once a week; clay-based to unblock pores or cream-based to enrich parched skin.

Exfoliators
Choose a fine-grained product with ingredients such as ground oats and seeds. Use twice-weekly to reveal healthy new skin.

Organic muslin cloths
These can be used to remove cleansers and masks, and to gently exfoliate.

A naturally healthy glow

Make-up, like skincare products, can also contain undesirable ingredients. Fortunately, natural cosmetic companies now offer us the same standard of colour and coverage without the unnecessary chemicals. Formulations have improved and products are available for all skin types and tones, from sparkly eye shadows to organic creamy lipsticks.

Look for brands that are pushing the boundaries, using recycled packaging and renewable energy in their production. We chose Elysambre (www.elysambre.com) for most of the bridal looks in this book. It offers refillable containers for all its cosmetics, which are both eco-friendly and super stylish. For more ideas visit www.theremustbeabetterway.co.uk, www.naturisimo.com, www.greenorganics.com.au or www.futurenatural.com.

Getting the best from eco make-up

* Apply an organic moisturiser to prime the skin ready for a natural mineral-based foundation.
* When using a matt lipstick, apply organic lip balm afterwards to help it set and minimise dry patches. Apply lip balm before lipstick for a sheer look.
* Natural mascara is not waterproof but will suit contact lens wearers and is easy to remove.
* Curl eyelashes before applying mascara to make your eyes appear bigger and lashes longer.
* Check your make-up from the side using a hand-held mirror in daylight, to see the photographer's view.

Animal testing

It is widely acknowledged that it is not ethically acceptable to test either products or ingredients on animals, but unfortunately it still happens. Truly natural skincare companies only test their ranges on human volunteers. Vegan brides should check if products contain beeswax.

Blemishes

If you develop a spot the night before the wedding, cleanse your face, pat dry with a clean towel and apply neat tea tree essential oil to the blemish with a cotton bud. Before bed, change your pillowcase for a clean one, as it could harbour blemish-creating bacteria. To reduce the chance of spots before the big day, take these small steps:

* Drink plenty of water in the preceding months.
* Follow a balanced organic diet.
* Keep stress levels low.
* Change your pillowcases twice-weekly.
* Find a natural skincare regime that suits you and follow it religiously.
* Always remove make-up before bed.

Puffy eyes

If you wake on the wedding day with puffy eyes, place either a slice of fresh organic cucumber or a cool, wet chamomile tea bag on each eye for five minutes.

Miracle creams

Fruit acid face masks or oil-rich balms are the perfect pre-wedding skin savers (never use clay-based masks on the day). Simply apply on the morning of the wedding, following the instructions, for smooth, photo-ready skin. Follow with an anti-wrinkle cream to help minimise the appearance of fine lines and prep your face for make-up. My favourites are:

❊ Logona Wrinkle Therapy Fluid – a miracle cream that erases lines before your very eyes.

❊ Nude Skincare Miracle Mask – so simple to use, with fantastic line-reducing results.

❊ REN Glycolactic Skin Renewal Peel Mask – an exfoliating mask to improve skin tone and firmness.

❊ Neal's Yard Remedies Wild Rose Beauty Balm – this fragrant balm reduces fine lines, boosts radiance and softens dry skin.

Karen and Lee, of
Lee Matthews Studio,
have created striking
hair and make-up styles
for this book.

Be stress free

Wedding planning can be stressful, however organised you are. I've included these relaxing tips to help keep your stress levels down and your energy high. Allow yourself an hour a week to unwind and pamper your body and soul. Play soothing music and light candles to create a warm, calming atmosphere.

Aromatherapy oils

Essential oils extracted from plants and flowers can balance, relax or energise. You can use them in an oil burner, in the bath, or for massage. All these methods can have positive effects on the senses, nervous system and skin. Never apply direct to the skin (except for tea tree oil on spots, see page 176); always dilute in a carrier such as almond oil first. Pregnant women should consult an aromatherapist before using any essential oils.

Flower remedies

These are useful for emotional upset and stress. Bach Remedies are made from British flowers and Bush Remedies from Australian plants. The best known is Bach Rescue Remedy, a multi-purpose remedy that is valuable after an accident, shock or upset, and also for nerves. Carry it with you during the planning stage and on the wedding day, just in case. My favourite individual remedy is White Chestnut. This helps to quieten an active mind at night, when your thoughts are swimming with invitations and colour schemes.

DIY spa treats

You can easily replicate many therapeutic spa treatments at home with a few simple ingredients. Look for oils, dried flowers and herbs in high-street natural beauty shops such as Neal's Yard Remedies. Try the ideas below with your groom, mum or bridesmaids.

Facials

A monthly facial will improve the health of your skin and help it glow. First, apply cleanser and slowly massage into the skin using small circular motions. Finish each circuit of the face with a gentle press on the temples. Once rinsed, apply a face mask, avoiding the eye area. Pop fresh slices of cooled cucumber over your eyes, sit back and relax for ten minutes – enjoy a warm herbal tea for maximum therapeutic effect.

Remove the mask with a warm muslin cloth and splash your face ten times with fresh, cold water to close the pores. Then, using a few drops of organic facial oil, gently massage, following the contours of the face. Finally, apply a small amount of eye gel or cream to the eye area using small patting motions with your ring finger.

Wedding planner tip:
To help essential oils to disperse in bath water, mix a few drops into a tablespoon of milk first.

Body scrub

For baby-soft skin, make a paste from three tablespoons of olive oil, a couple of drops of essential oil, a teaspoon of runny honey and a handful of either sugar, salt or coarse oats (avoid salt if you have sensitive skin). Rub lightly on to dry skin, paying attention to elbows but avoiding the face. Rinse off with warm water and pat skin dry. Follow with a rich organic body cream or oil.

Bath soak

For a relaxing and skin-softening bath, place a handful each of oats, dried marigolds and lavender or rose petals in a muslin cloth. Tie into a ball and place under the hot tap while you run the bath. Let the herbs infuse in the water and add a tablespoon of fairtrade shea nut butter.

And breathe...

If you are about to make a speech or walk down the aisle and are feeling a little anxious, take three deep breaths. This will help you to relax and give you a confidence boost. Similarly, if you are having difficulty sleeping and switching off, concentrate and breathe in gently for a count of seven, then breathe out for a count of eleven. Repeat until you feel more relaxed.

Stress-busting essential oils

❉ Chamomile – a heavenly scent, and deeply relaxing. Blend with lavender and rose in a bath before bedtime for a good night's sleep.

❉ Geranium – a balancing oil, useful when you feel out of sorts. Blend with rose to enhance your mood.

❉ Jasmine – when things get tough, choose sweet-smelling jasmine to bring a sense of renewed optimism.

❉ Rose – if you feel weepy from emotional stress, the scent of rose can help keep tears at bay. Plus it smells divine.

Edible face masks

These face and hand treatments are all made using ingredients found in your fridge, garden or greengrocer's. Choose organic fruits to minimise exposure to pesticides. Afterwards, relax with a lavender eye mask.

STRAWBERRY EXFOLIATING MASK

1 tomato

3 strawberries

1 teaspoon of manuka honey

Chop the tomato finely and mash with the strawberries and honey. Apply to damp skin, avoiding the eye area, and leave for 5 minutes. Rinse well and moisturise for silky-smooth, decongested skin.

AVOCADO, HONEY AND OATMEAL NOURISHING MASK

1 ripe avocado

1 teaspoon of manuka honey

1 teaspoon of fine ground oatmeal

Mash all the ingredients together and apply to clean, dry skin. Leave for 10 minutes and rinse off with plenty of water. Follow with a good natural moisturiser for soft, nourished skin.

TOMATO AND YOGURT HAND MASK

1 ripe tomato

1 small pot of natural yogurt

Mash the tomato and mix with the yogurt. Smooth the mixture on to dry, clean hands and leave for 30 minutes. Rinse well and apply hand cream.

LAVENDER EYE MASKS

These are perfect for soothing a stressed mind and also help to de-puff eyes. Take a piece of fabric and fold in half. Draw on the outline of an eye mask and cut out so you have two pieces the same. With right sides together, carefully stitch all the way around the edges, leaving a small hole about 2cm long. Turn the bag right side out and fill with dried lavender flowers. Sew up the hole and stitch a wide ribbon on to each side seam as a tie. Lie back, place the mask over your eyes and relax.

Hair and finishing touches

Organic natural shampoos, conditioners, hair masks and styling products now rival mainstream brands and keep your hair and scalp healthy without using synthetic chemicals. Choose your wedding day hairstyle with your dress in mind. With a floaty 1970s chiffon dress, flowing locks and a simple hair-band around the forehead are perfect, or try a daisy chain with long dresses that have simple lines. Structured modern gowns favour an amazing up-do, while vintage skirt suits look stunning with short hair. Pretty antique tiaras and homemade flower corsages complement most styles and can lift a look with minimal effort.

For shiny, conditioned hair, work in a tablespoon of pure coconut oil, wrap your hair up in a towel and leave for an hour. Then massage neat shampoo into the hair before adding water to create a lather. Rinse with plenty of warm water and dry as normal.

Teeth and tans

Book a dental check-up at least a month before the wedding, to allow enough time for any work you may need. Rather than having teeth chemically whitened, make a 'clean and polish' appointment with a hygienist three days before your wedding.

Fake tans have become a popular preparation for the big day. You can now find natural fake tans in both cream and spray applications. Exfoliating thoroughly beforehand and moisturising well afterwards will help them last.

Nails

Most nail varnishes contain toxic chemicals such as formaldehyde. A few companies have developed kinder alternatives, in fabulous colours such as vintage rose and hot pink. Either choose a brand such as Zoya or Butter London, which are toluene, formaldehyde and DBP free, or, alternatively, shine your nails with a buffing board for a polished look without varnish.

Natural perfumes

Scents are notorious for containing many synthetic chemicals. Happily, companies such as Jo Wood Organics are producing organic eaux de toilette, while Florascent uses natural essences. Robert Tisserand's *The Art of Aromatherapy* tells you how to make flower waters – my tip is to put flower water in an atomiser with a drop of the same flower essential oil to accentuate the scent.

Time out for the two of you

It is important that you and your groom have time for each other in the run-up to the big day. In the final weeks a wedding can become time-consuming, so my firm advice is that you take at least a day off each week to relax and enjoy each other's company, with no mention of the wedding. This ensures that you remain focused on why you are marrying and don't exhaust yourselves.

Beauty must-haves for the big day

❋ DIY mineral water spray – decant local mineral water into a small bottle with an atomiser top. Use during the day to refresh skin; it also helps to 'set' make-up.

❋ Small make-up kit containing natural lipstick, lip balm and powder.

❋ Organic tissues to keep shine under control.

❋ A small deodorant stone (available from health-food shops and natural pharmacies). These leave no stains and are completely natural.

❋ Aloe vera gel. In summer, arm yourself with a parasol to keep shaded, but if your skin is exposed to the sun, aloe will soothe it and reduce redness.

DIY hair top tips

❊ Make your own salt spray by dissolving sea salt in boiled water. Spray on to damp hair and style for a tousled, fashionable matt finish. Ideal for a beach wedding.

❊ Decorate your hair with small fresh flowers (your florist can provide these on clips). Alternatively, try tiny vintage corsages and fine hair-bands for 1950s chic.

❊ Be comfortable on the day. If you usually wear your hair loose, don't feel pressured to have it up.

❊ If you are home-styling your hair, have a couple of trial runs and take photographs from the front, side and back to remind you of what works.

❊ Choose a natural, non-aerosol hairspray to set your up-do.

Lee has used hellebores to dress Karen's hair. Hand-finished couture silk gown by Jessica Charleston.

* *Your wedding day*
My essential wedding kit and tips for an enjoyable day, including the art of delegation.

* *Bridesmaid's tote bag*
An easy-to-sew pattern that can be a thank-you gift and hold all their little essentials.

* *Saving memories*
And making a memorable exit.

* *After the party*
Recycling waste, gifting flowers and composting.

* *Green honeymoons*
Adventures for the bride and groom, from luxury eco hotels to volunteering.

The Big Day

You've searched out the best in eco and organic suppliers, handmade your invites, cake or favours, chosen gorgeous seasonal flowers and local food, and revived an exquisite vintage dress. And now the big day has finally arrived. In this chapter you'll find tips on how to enjoy your wedding, as well as essential information on fabulous earth-friendly honeymoons.

Enjoying your day

Planning a wedding is time-consuming and requires considerable effort. You may have spent months, even years, preparing for your perfect big day, and carefully choosing your green products and services. And the bulk of this work usually falls on the bride. The result is a day to which a great deal of expectation is attached.

The anticipation of a wedding can be delightful, but can also bring stress and worry. In my experience, the best advice I can give to brides is to relax on the day and go with the flow. Small things may go wrong – a guest might be late or you may mark your dress – but these tiny annoyances are unimportant. The reason you are holding a wedding is to be married; the party is a nice aside. So be happy, smile, relax into your day and enjoy every minute, as it will fly past in no time.

Keep your sense of humour

A bride once phoned me the day before her wedding in an absolute panic. She was beside herself: something terrible had happened, and she had no idea what to do. "Louise, you have to help me," she pleaded.

It turned out that her dog had eaten all her artisan chocolate favours, handmade boxes and all. This was a lifelong friend, so I instantly knew what to do. I laughed. And the minute I laughed, so did she. In that moment she realised that this wasn't the end of the world; it wouldn't stop the wedding. New favours were made, the guests loved the story, and we still laugh about it to this day.

Delegation

On-the-day delegation is an important part of pre-wedding planning. If you are employing the services of an eco wedding planner, you won't need this, but if not, it helps to have friends on standby for specific tasks. Write each person a list so they understand what is required. If they are responsible for checking that suppliers have arrived, make sure they have the correct contact details.

Husband and wife

After the ceremony, try to have at least ten minutes alone together away from the hustle and bustle of the party. You will be entertaining your guests for the rest of the day so programme in time that is just for the two of you.

Inclement weather

Be prepared and take a golfing umbrella and wellies. Wind and rain can, however, make for dramatic outdoor photos – bride and groom under an umbrella with veil flying in the breeze. If you laugh about it you will feel much better.

Wedding planner tip:
Remember to talk to your groom! It is easy to spend all your time speaking with your guests instead, but remember it is your day.

Bridesmaid's tote bag

This tote is a great thank-you gift and uses any fabrics you have to hand. It looks pretty with a complementary, paler lining. Fill with on-the-day essentials to make bridesmaids feel appreciated.

YOU WILL NEED:

2 pieces of fabric at least 40cm by 90cm

A piece of fabric 1m by 16cm for the handle

Measuring tape, tailor's chalk and fabric scissors

Ribbons and lace

Vintage buttons

Needle, pins and matching thread

Sewing machine (not essential)

METHOD:

1. Draw 4 rectangles measuring 40cm by 45cm on your material – 2 on each pattern of fabric if you are using a different lining material. Cut out.

2. Take the piece that will be the outside front and stitch ribbons and lace on top to make a design (see the photograph, above right).

3. Pin the front and back outside pieces together, right sides facing inwards, and stitch along three sides to form a bag shape.

4. Repeat with the two lining pieces, this time leaving a 5cm gap in the seam.

5. Pinch out the bottom two corners of the outer bag and stitch horizontally across each corner so it forms an equal triangle. Repeat with the lining bag.

6. Cut two further pieces of fabric 1m long by 8cm wide for the handle. Pin them together, right sides inwards, and stitch together down each long side. Turn the handle the right way out.

7. Turn the outer layer of the bag right way out and place it inside the lining so that the right sides of the fabric face each other.

8. Tuck the handle in between the bags so it falls in a loop at the bottom and line up the edges of the handle between the raw seams on each side.

9. Stitch together at the top edge all the way round.

10. Turn the bag the right way out by pulling all the fabric, including the handle, through the hole in the lining.

11. Sew up the hole, pushing the lining back down into the outer bag, and shake.

12. Embellish with a pin-on corsage (see page 68).

Wedding planner tip:
Press the seams as you go along for a crisp, professional finish, then lightly press the whole bag at the end.

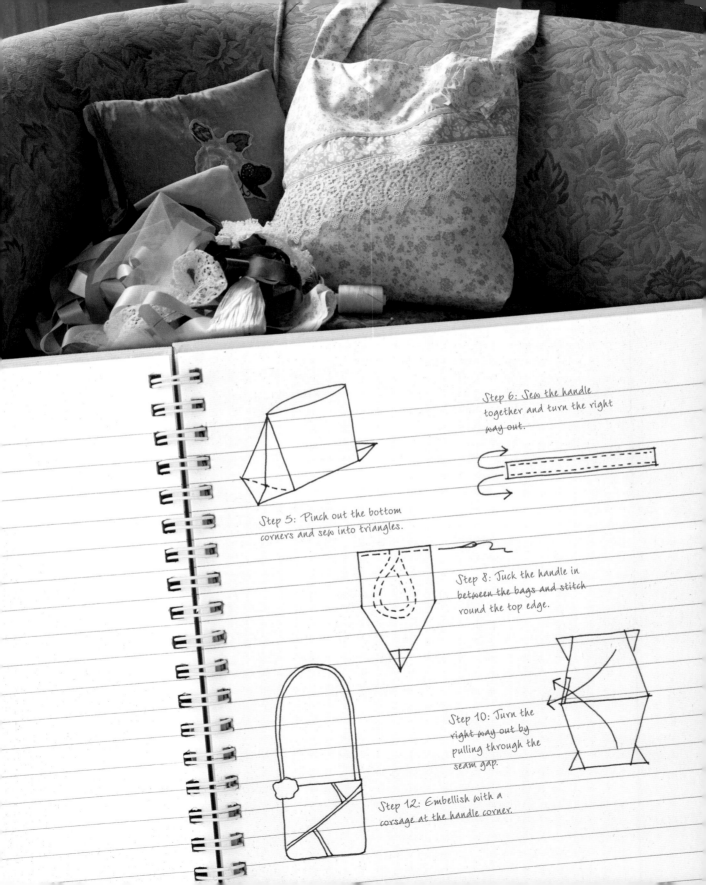

Step 6: Sew the handle together and turn the right way out.

Step 5: Pinch out the bottom corners and sew into triangles.

Step 8: Tuck the handle in between the bags and stitch round the top edge.

Step 10: Turn the right way out by pulling through the seam gap.

Step 12: Embellish with a corsage at the handle corner.

After the wedding

It is a fashionable custom to leave your reception before it ends, and go straight on honeymoon. Whether a snug bed and breakfast a mile down the road or a train ride to somewhere you've never explored, it is fun to dress for the occasion. If you love vintage, why not invest in an original 1950s frock and vanity case for your trip, and enjoy filling the case with natural and organic treats.

Wedding memories

Keep tokens from your day as mementoes, and gather them into an antique box or handmade album. A pressed flower from your bouquet, place card, bottle label or cork, pebble, dried leaf, order of service, handful of confetti and speeches can all be saved and enjoyed for years to come.

The post-party clean-up

Delegate post-party tasks to your good friends, so you don't have to worry. Here are a few tips to get them started:

❉ Provide marked recycling bins for paper, cans, food waste and plastics.

❉ Try to use cardboard boxes or biodegradable corn starch bags to collect waste.

❉ Collect any spare toys, games and non-perishable favours, and take them to a local charity shop.

❉ To make distribution of floral displays easy, write a note on the place name cards of the guests you would like them to go to, so they can take them home. Alternatively, hold a 'raffle' using the place cards.

❉ Ask the venue managers if there is a compost bin for food and floral waste.

❉ If you are having a beach, park or garden wedding, ask a few friends to litter-pick to ensure you don't leave any trace.

❉ Allocate one person to oversee the return of hired items such as furniture and suits the following day.

Maya & Marc

ARE
TYING THE KNOT
-
CEREMONY AT
3.00PM
(PLEASE ARRIVE AT 2.30)
IN THE OCTAGON
THE ASSEMBLY ROOMS
-
CELEBRATIONS COMMENCE
WITH DRINKS IN THE CARD ROOM
FOLLOWED BY
AN EVENING RECEPTION
IN THE TEA ROOM
WITH
FOOD, MUSIC, DANCING
&
LOTS OF CAKE

SATURDAY 7TH FEBRUARY 200
at the Assembly Rooms
BENNETT ST
BATH
BA1 2QH

UNTIL MIDNIGHT

Good morning

If you and your guests are staying the night, continue the celebrations the following morning with a big, organic breakfast. Make the most of a kata tipi or yurt by eating together inside before the tent is dismantled.

Your honeymoon

The choice of eco-aware honeymoon possibilities is endless, whether volunteering in Eastern Europe or luxuriating at an eco spa. Consider 'slow' travel and ethical options to minimise your impact.

Organic bed and breakfast and eco hotels

Think about staying close to home. You can find environmentally aware and organic bed and breakfast retreats for many countries in *Alastair Sawday's Green Places to Stay* (www.sawdays.co.uk). Spend a day beachcombing, then head back for dinner in front of a log fire. Sample delicious local breakfasts and natural bathroom treats while wrapped in an organic cotton bathrobe. What could be better?

For luxurious organic spa days and Michelin-starred food, try an eco hotel from the sites in the Directory, with gorgeous natural furnishings and modern green gadgets.

Honeymooning on a shoestring

Backpacking, hiking, house-swapping, camping – you can have a dream holiday spending very little. If you crave luxury, book a weekend in an eco boutique hotel. Alternatively, many organic farms now have permanent yurt fields, with proper beds and warm blankets. Zac and I spent a fabulous shoestring break in Venice, camping at Marina de Venezia next to miles of sandy private beach. By day we took the boat across to Venice; in the evenings we barbecued at the campsite and watched the sun go down together.

Festivals

These can offer distinctive accommodation as well as music and atmosphere. Glastonbury, for example, has private tipis in the festival fields or luxurious shikar tents on the outskirts, complete with butlers and private bar. Festivals are held across the globe; choosing one local to you will help to keep down your carbon footprint.

Eco tourism

You may have been dreaming about and saving for your honeymoon for years, and looking forward to relaxing and exploring somewhere different. There are many eco-friendly places to stay worldwide, from safari lodges in Africa to snorkelling in tropical blue seas. Avoid large chain hotels and instead choose local independents that work hard to protect the environment and benefit their neighbouring society. Visit www.ecotourism.org for more information.

Slow travel

Go slow and choose more sustainable transport such as bus, train and passenger boat. Not only will you use less carbon, you will see more of the country. If you have to go by air, then offset your flight through a reputable carbon offset programme.

Volunteering holidays

Adventurous couples could join a volunteering holiday with international charity the British Trust for Conservation (BTCV). It offers expeditions across the globe, carrying out important conservation work. Whether restoring forests in Cameroon, repairing mountain trails in Iceland, or building nesting sites for wild birds in Bulgaria, you will have fun while helping the environment. See www.btcv.org.uk.

Wedding planner tip:
Pack lavender essential oil to treat mosquito bites, citronella oil to repel insects and aloe vera gel to soothe sun-exposed skin.

Easy eco packing

A friend once told me the golden rule with packing is to lay everything you plan to take on your bed and then halve it.

❋ Pack items that have more than one use. Linen kaftans are the perfect beach cover-up, make a pretty top with jeans, or can be teamed with a belt for an evening dress.

❋ Tie square vintage silk scarves at the neck, use as a bikini top, or wrap around your head in hot sun.

❋ Always pack an eco bag such as an Onya (www.onyabags.com). Ideal for shopping, the beach, or even sitting on.

❋ Vintage clothing can be a pleasure to pack, as it is often made with fabrics that don't crease easily.

❋ Take a vacuum flask or mug to minimise paper cup and bottle waste.

❋ Remember a natural SPF sun cream such as Lavera Faces SPF 15.

Natural Wedding Planner

This planner is based on the main stages of organising your wedding, rather than a specific timeline. Some couples may have years to plan their wedding, while others may only have a few weeks. You may not need all the elements below – many will only apply to larger weddings – so simply choose which are relevant and tick them off as they are done.

Stage 1 – The exciting bit

This stage can take as long as you want it to. But remember that some popular venues and churches need to be booked well in advance.

Start compiling your wedding notebook (never too early) with ideas for your natural day (see page 32) ☐

Choose your wedding date ☐

Decide the type of ceremony you would like (see page 30) ☐

Consider how many guests will attend ☐

Look at the seasonal flowers and produce available at the time of your wedding (see the seasonal calendars on pages 218 and 219) ☐

Select and book the venue for your ceremony (if required, meet with the vicar, priest or minister) ☐

Select and book the venue for your reception (after visiting different options) ☐

Choose your best man and chief bridesmaid, if appropriate ☐

Hire a tipi or marquee and furniture ☐

Buy wedding insurance, if it is a large wedding ☐

Decide on your wedding gift or charity list ☐

Make wildflower seed paper for invites, decorations and favour boxes (see page 94) ☐

Order or make your invitations ☐

Launch your wedding website ☐

Send out invitations or e-vites ☐

Start your natural skincare regime ☐

Stage 2 – Bride and groom

Enjoy spending time with your groom on these elements – they are all the personal aspects of your day.

Shop for or make your dress ☐

Find your bridal accessories and make your dress corsage (see page 68) ☐

Book your honeymoon (if you need your passports, make sure they are valid) ☐

Book first-night accommodation (if you are not going straight on honeymoon or staying at the venue) ☐

Choose your groom's outfit ☐

Source accessories for the groom ☐

Shop for wedding rings, or have an existing ring reworked (see page 79) ☐

Sew your wedding day bag (see page 88) ☐

Choose your first dance song ☐

Discuss the ceremony music, hymns, vows, poetry and readings ☐

Stage 3 – Suppliers

Some suppliers will get booked up quickly, especially photographers. If you are planning on a handmade or DIY day this stage might take a little longer.

Book a photographer and discuss the shots you would like ☐

Book a DJ or compile your iPod playlist, or hire musicians ☐

Book hair and make-up appointments, or decide on a style to do yourself ☐

Book a caterer, or decide on your own homemade menu ☐

Make chutneys a few weeks beforehand, so they can mature (see page 114) ☐

Hire crockery, cutlery and serving dishes, if required ☐

Collect hampers and crates to transport outdoor food, if required ☐

Book a florist, or attend a floristry workshop ☐

Book transport, if required – rickshaws, red buses, tandems ☐

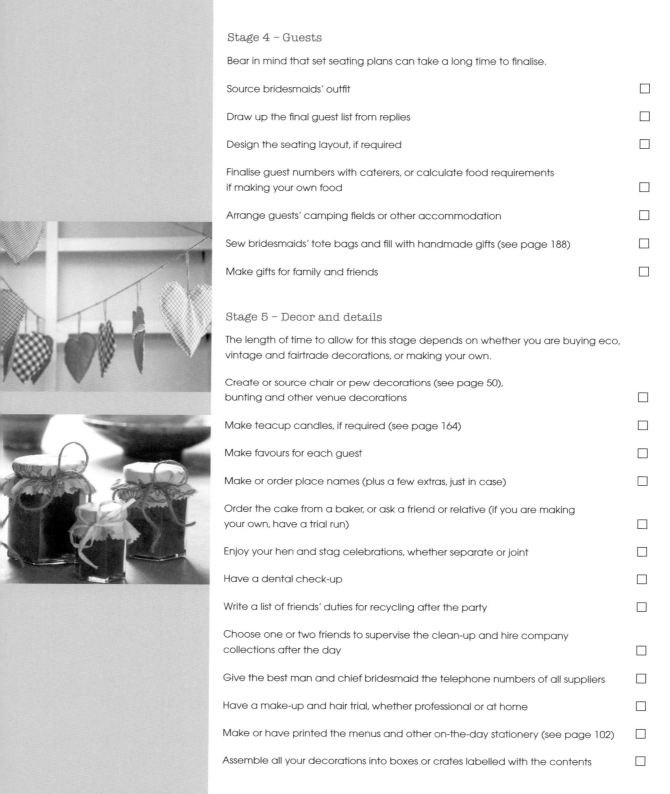

Stage 4 – Guests

Bear in mind that set seating plans can take a long time to finalise.

Source bridesmaids' outfit ☐

Draw up the final guest list from replies ☐

Design the seating layout, if required ☐

Finalise guest numbers with caterers, or calculate food requirements
if making your own food ☐

Arrange guests' camping fields or other accommodation ☐

Sew bridesmaids' tote bags and fill with handmade gifts (see page 188) ☐

Make gifts for family and friends ☐

Stage 5 – Decor and details

The length of time to allow for this stage depends on whether you are buying eco,
vintage and fairtrade decorations, or making your own.

Create or source chair or pew decorations (see page 50),
bunting and other venue decorations ☐

Make teacup candles, if required (see page 164) ☐

Make favours for each guest ☐

Make or order place names (plus a few extras, just in case) ☐

Order the cake from a baker, or ask a friend or relative (if you are making
your own, have a trial run) ☐

Enjoy your hen and stag celebrations, whether separate or joint ☐

Have a dental check-up ☐

Write a list of friends' duties for recycling after the party ☐

Choose one or two friends to supervise the clean-up and hire company
collections after the day ☐

Give the best man and chief bridesmaid the telephone numbers of all suppliers ☐

Have a make-up and hair trial, whether professional or at home ☐

Make or have printed the menus and other on-the-day stationery (see page 102) ☐

Assemble all your decorations into boxes or crates labelled with the contents ☐

Stage 6 – The week before

It's important to set time aside to relax during this stage, so you don't burn out.

Haircuts for bride and groom ☐

Write speeches ☐

Final dress fitting, if necessary ☐

Break in your shoes ☐

Order your flowers, if not using a florist ☐

Check you have something, old, new, borrowed and blue ☐

Bake your own cake or cupcakes (see pages 124 and 128) ☐

Prepare your own food with family and friends ☐

Pack your wedding day kit (see page 186) ☐

Pack your honeymoon bags (remember your passport) ☐

Confirm all suppliers by telephone ☐

Tell the best man which suppliers need to be paid in cash on the day
and give him the correct money in named envelopes ☐

Stage 7 – The day before

If it is a hot day, remember to keep out of the sun to avoid tan lines or burning.

Decorate the marquee or venue with friends and family ☐

Tie your bridal bouquet, if your are making it yourself – keep it somewhere
cool and dark ☐

Ask a friend to transport your cake, if homemade, to the venue ☐

Give yourself a home manicure ☐

Enjoy a relaxed dinner with friends ☐

Wash your hair ☐

Add any extras to your wedding day kit, such as your speech or family gifts ☐

Give your bridesmaids their thank-you tote bags filled with
little handmade gifts and treats ☐

On the day

This really is the best bit – enjoy every minute. Smile, whatever the weather – it's your wedding day!

Enjoy a relaxing bath or shower with aromatic natural bath products ☐

Eat a little breakfast, even if you don't feel like it ☐

Arrange to have a gift or note delivered to your groom as a surprise ☐

Have hair and make-up done, or do it yourself ☐

Enjoy spending time with your bridesmaids ☐

Ask a bridesmaid to make fresh petal confetti from roses
(this takes minutes – see page 152) ☐

Get dressed an hour before you are due to leave, to allow time for fabulous photos ☐

Take your bouquet out of water 30 minutes before you leave for the ceremony
and pat the stems dry ☐

Have a happy wedding and enjoy your day! ☐

After the wedding

Enjoy your eco honeymoon with your husband!

Post out thank-you cards or emails ☐

Dry your bouquet as a memento of the day ☐

Look forward to seeing the beautiful photos ☐

Important for all weddings

Obtain written quotations for any suppliers or services.

Book everything in writing and keep the letters or emails together somewhere safe.

Pay deposits for suppliers on time.

Keep receipts for any payments made.

Remember to have time off from the wedding planning – at least one day a week should be wedding free. Go out, fly a kite, walk the dog and relax.

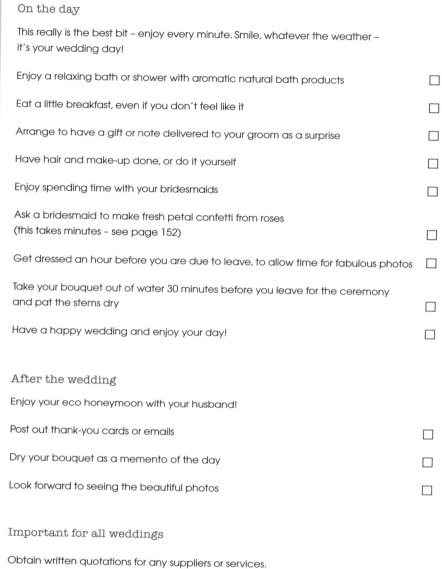

This is a selection of my favourite books, for natural wedding reading. Some of them relate to weddings and honeymoons and some do not, but all are useful and interesting to leaf through, look at and keep by for tips.

Venue and travel guides

The Alastair Sawday guides:
Eat Slow Britain
Go Slow England
Green Places to Stay
Special Places: Venues in Britain

Eco Hotels of the World, Alex Conti
Ecoescape – Responsible Escapism in the UK,
Laura Burgess
The Guardian Green Travel Guide, edited by Liane Katz
Organic Places to Stay, Linda Moss

Cooking, growing and picking your own

Cake Chic, Peggy Porschen
Cakes for Romantic Occasions,
May Clee-Cadman
The Complete Gardener, Monty Don
The Dairy Book of Family Cookery, Alexandra Artley
Encyclopedia of Organic Gardening, HDRA
*Favourite Country Preserves – Traditional Home-made
Jam, Chutney and Pickle Recipes*, Carol Wilson
Flower Course, Jane Packer
*The Forager Handbook – A Guide to the Edible Plants
of Britain*, Miles Irving
*How to Store Your Garden Produce – The Key to
Self-sufficiency*, Piers Warren and Tessa Pettingell
The International Book of Sugarcraft (Books 1 and 2),
Nicholas Lodge and Janice Murfitt
Jekka's Complete Herb Book, Jekka McVicar
The Little Book of Organic Farming,
The Soil Association
Seasonal Preserves, Joanna Farrow
Seasonal Wreaths and Bouquets, Paula Pryke
Sugar Flowers for Cake Decorating, Alan Dunn
Your Organic Allotment, Pauline Pears and Ian Spence

Handmade and DIY

Creative Handmade Paper, David Watson
Knitting in No Time, Melody Griffiths
Loop Pretty Knits, Susan Cropper
Paper Making with Garden Plants and Common Weeds,
Helen Heibert

*Printing by Hand – A Modern Guide to Printing with
Handmade Stamps, Stencils, and Silk Screens*,
Lena Corwin
*Sew It Up – A Modern Manual of Practical and Decorative
Sewing Techniques*, Ruth Singer
Wedding Invitations, Jennifer Cegielski

Vintage and shopping

*Alligators, Old Mink and New Money –
One Woman's Adventures in Vintage Clothing*,
Alison Houtte and Melissa Houtte
It's Vintage, Darling! – How To Be a Clothes Connoisseur,
Christa Weil
*The Little Guide to Vintage Shopping – Insider Tips,
Helpful Hints, Hip Shops*, Melody Fortier
*Making Vintage Bags – 20 Original Sewing Patterns for
Vintage Bags and Purses*, Emma Brennan
The Rough Guide to Ethical Shopping,
Duncan Clark
*Secondhand Chic – Finding Fabulous Fashion at
Consignment, Vintage, and Thrift Stores*, Christa Weil
*Shopping for Vintage – The Definitive
Guide to Vintage Fashion*, Funmi Odulate
*Vintage Fashion – Collecting and Wearing Designer
Classics*, Carlton Books
Vintage Handbags, Marnie Fogg
Vintage Shoes, Caroline Cox

Natural beauty

The Art of Aromatherapy, Robert B Tisserand
The Green Beauty Bible, Sarah Stacey and
Josephine Fairley
Natural Health and Bodycare Book,
Neal's Yard Remedies
The Practice of Aromatherapy, Dr Jean Valnet
Recipes for Natural Beauty, Neal's Yard Remedies
Vogue Natural Health and Beauty, Bronwen Meredith

Eco, ethical and thrifty

Ms Harris's Book of Green Household Management,
Caroline Harris
The Thrift Book, India Knight
What's in This Stuff?, Pat Thomas

Natural Wedding Directory

Legalities

www.direct.gov.uk
Look in the Government, citizens and rights section for information about marriages and civil partnerships, and overseas marriages.

www.adviceguide.org.uk
The Family section has details for England, Scotland, Wales and Northern Ireland.

Venues

The West Country and southwest of England have a larger choice of eco venues, but there is a growing number elsewhere, too.

www.battlesteads.com
An 18th-century Northumberland inn with woodchip boiler and its own home-grown produce.

www.bathvenues.co.uk
Home of Bath's famous Roman Baths and Assembly Rooms.

www.bedruthan.com
The Bedruthan Steps is an eco hotel with stunning Cornish scenery.

www.beechenhill.co.uk
Organic farm in the Derbyshire Peak District.

www.clavelshaybarn.co.uk
An 18th-century barn in the Quantock Hills catering for small weddings.

www.coombefarmwoods.co.uk
Licensed Devon farmhouse and cider barn, with an oak tree in the woodland glade for alternative ceremonies.

www.cornishtipiholidays.co.uk
Acres of north Cornwall woodland, beautiful tipis and a wedding licence – what more could you need?

www.doddingtonhall.com
A stunning Elizabethan stately home near Lincoln, offering green weddings from June 2011.

www.follyfarm.org
A 250-acre nature reserve near Bristol, managed by the Avon Wildlife Trust.

www.forestry.gov.uk
Woodland weddings, from Westonbirt Arboretum in Gloucestershire to Caig Falls in Scotland.

www.forever-green.info
Seventy acres of Nottinghamshire woodland, plus locally sourced food.

www.halswell.co.uk
Historic Somerset country house available for hire.

www.huntstileorganicfarm.co.uk
Soil Association-certified farm in the Quantocks.

www.kew.org/venues
The UNESCO world heritage site and home to the Royal Botanic Gardens offers London venues from the Orangery to the Palace Pavilion Marquee, plus Wakehurst Place in West Sussex, a stately home with arboretum.

www.lakewoodcentre.co.uk
A carbon-neutral eco barn near Bristol, with local food and spectacular views.

www.longhouseweddings.co.uk
Award-winning eco venue at the Mill on the Brue in the heart of Somerset.

www.matara.co.uk
Beautiful green venue set in 28 acres of parkland in Gloucestershire, offering unique and special celebrations.

www.oldpines.co.uk
Small Scottish hotel with its own reedbed and views of Ben Nevis.

www.penpont.com
Grade I-listed house and outbuildings with beautiful grounds and Soil Association-certified organic kitchen garden, near Brecon.

www.penrhos.com
Romantic, 13th-century Herefordshire manor with organic food.

www.pinescalyx.co.uk
Sustainable, low-carbon licensed venue in Kent, with sea views.

www.rockseast.org.uk
More than 100 acres of woodland near Bath, and plenty of space for giant hat kata tipis.

www.scarlethotel.co.uk
Cornwall's best eco boutique hotel.

www.sheepdroveweddings.co.uk
A beautiful eco-friendly building and organic farm in Berkshire.

www.south-farm.co.uk
Restored farm in South
Cambridgeshire, with organically
grown food and its own nature reserve.

www.stayinacastle.com
Eco boutique hotel at Augill Castle in
the Lake District.

www.thegreenhousehotel.co.uk
Eco-conscious contemporary
boutique hotel in Bournemouth.

www.thornburycastle.co.uk
Tudor castle in Gloucestershire with
vineyard.

www.winkworthfarm.com
Organic farm in the Cotswolds, with
renovated eco-friendly barns and
local suppliers.

www.woodbrooke.org.uk
A Quaker centre set in tranquil
grounds in Birmingham, in the
former family home of chocolate
maker George Cadbury.

Venue and green wedding guides

www.ecofriendlyweddings.co.uk
UK and international directory of
suppliers, including venues.

www.ecohotelsoftheworld.com
Eco boutique hotels, guest houses,
farms and spas worldwide.

www.greenunion.co.uk
Includes a directory of suppliers, from
venues to dresses.

www.organicholidays.co.uk
International website of Organic
Places to Stay.

www.sawdays.co.uk
Search the Ethical Collection on
Alastair Sawday's Special Places
website for bed and breakfast, hotel
and self-catering in the UK and further
afield. With wedding venues, check
for the leaf symbol, which shows their
environmental efforts.

www.theecologist.org
Not a wedding site, but a great
resource on eco living.

www.thenaturalweddingbook.com
The website of this book.

**www.thenaturalweddingcompany.
co.uk**
A helpful resource and directory
(not to be confused with *The Natural
Wedding Book*'s own site, above).

Marquee, yurt and tipi hire

Most of these companies will deliver
nationwide, but to reduce 'tent miles'
choose a supplier near your venue.

www.bambootents.com
Unusual tents with eco-friendly
bamboo frames, from near Oxford.

www.bedouintents.com
Sumptuous, ornate, decorative tents.

www.cruckmarquee.co.uk
Traditional English timber-framed,
open-sided marquees.

www.overthemoontents.co.uk
Yurts, tipis, vintage marquees and
medieval pavilions.

www.papakata.co.uk
Home of the fabulous kata tipi tent,
based near York.

www.peagreentoilets.co.uk
Greener mobile toilets.

www.redkiteyurts.com
Hand-crafted yurts from central
Scotland.

www.redtipi.co.uk
Graceful 'crow style' tipis from Sussex.

www.stunningtents.co.uk
Tipis, including giant hats, from a base
in Hampshire.

www.tfairloveyurts.co.uk
Devon company with a wide range
of yurts.

www.thunderboxes2go.co.uk
Mobile composting toilets.

www.tipis4hire.com
Fabulous tipis, large and small,
including big hat kata tipis, delivered
from Welwyn Garden City.

www.whitecanvastents.com
Beautiful Mughal-style marquees from
near Glastonbury.

www.yurtopia.co.uk
Handmade yurts from Sussex.

Dresses

www.beyondretro.com
Britain's largest vintage clothing
emporium, with shops in London and
Brighton, and also Sweden.

www.charlottecasadejus.com
Beautiful contemporary gowns made
from vintage fabrics.

www.ebay.co.uk
Find all you need.

www.elizabethavey.co.uk
London-based supplier of top-quality vintage dresses.

www.emmaembery.com
Bespoke dresses using vintage fabrics and hand embroidery, plus gorgeous ready-to-wear hair-bands and jewellery made from vintage elements.

www.freecycle.org
Sources of dresses and accessories, completely for free.

www.freudianslipsvintage.com
Award-winning online vintage boutique.

www.furcoatnoknickers.co.uk
Fabulous vintage dresses and accessories, plus made-to-measure dresses, based in Carnaby Street, central London.

www.heirloomcouture.com
Restoring, reinventing and recreating vintage dresses from their London studio.

www.ilovefreegle.org
UK-based alternative to Freecycle.

www.jessicacharleston.co.uk
The most exquisite dresses, lovingly handmade in Bath.

www.oxfam.co.uk/bridal
The original charity shop wedding dress suppliers.

www.queensofvintage.com
Online zine for lovers of vintage everywhere, including shop, exhibition and fair locations.

www.scarletvintage.co.uk
Bath-based boutique selling all things vintage.

www.stcatherinesfrome.co.uk/shops/make-mend
Make and Mend vintage shop with seamstresses in Frome, Somerset.

www.tammam.co.uk
Eco and ethical dress designer, who uses only organic, natural and peace fabrics, vintage trimmings and fairtrade practices.

www.thevintageweddingdresscompany.co.uk
An amazing collection of high-quality vintage dresses, based in London and recommended by *Vogue*.

www.wickedladycollectables.co.uk
Vintage dress patterns and shoes.

Eco fabrics, trimmings and natural dyes

www.aurorasilk.com
Peace silk and naturally dyed fabrics.

www.donnaflower.com
Vintage and retro fabrics, from 19th century to 1980s.

www.greenfibres.co.uk
Eco-friendly fabrics, from bamboo to nettle.

www.hempfabric.co.uk
Hemp, bamboo, linen and soy.

www.nearseanaturals.com
Not just fabrics, but organic braids, thread and lace.

www.oldfashionedstuff.co.uk
Vintage trimmings and buttons.

www.pure-tinctoria.co.uk
Natural dyes and naturally dyed yarns.

www.ragrescue.co.uk
Vintage fabrics and patchwork, plus lace and ribbons.

www.thehouseofhemp.co.uk
Hemp yarns.

www.wellcultivated.co.uk
Bamboo fabrics, including satin, and a great blog on eco materials.

Accessories

www.beyondskin.co.uk
Glamorous cruelty-free, vegan, handmade footwear.

www.ellandcee.co.uk
Silk undies and boudoir wear handmade in the UK.

www.enamore.co.uk
Ethical undies and accessories fashioned from vintage, natural and ethical fabrics.

www.louisebroad.co.uk
Romantic and stylish handmade hair accessories and wraps, using sheer silk and merino.

www.milliondesign.com
Handmade accessories with original vintage gems.

www.steptoesantiques.co.uk
Vintage bags, accessories and jewellery.

www.terraplana.co.uk
Fabulous ethical shoes for any occasion.

www.vintageatgoodwood.co.uk
A new festival celebrating all things vintage.

Jewellery

www.alfiesantiques.com
Established London antiques centre
with online shop.

www.aprildoubleday.com
Ethical rings using fairtrade metals
with Canadian gems.

www.coralquay.co.uk
Fairtrade beaded jewellery.

www.credjewellery.com
The original fairtrade jeweller.

www.fifibijoux.co.uk
Gorgeous ethical jewellery, including
wedding rings.

www.ingleandrhode.co.uk
Jewellery made using clean gold
and conflict-free diamonds.

www.kazuribeads.co.uk
Brightly coloured handmade
and fairtrade beads.

www.leblas.com
Made using recycled metals and
conflict-free gems.

www.magpievintage.co.uk
Vintage and reworked jewellery.

www.nessbirdjewellery1.
moonfruit.com
Handmade rings crafted with
fairtrade, recycled and ethically
sourced materials.

www.seaglass.co.uk
Unusual natural creations made from
salvaged sea glass.

www.thewoodhut.co.uk
Wooden rings crafted using local
British hardwoods.

www.weddingringworkshop.co.uk
Spend a day making your own
wedding rings.

www.woodenrings.co.uk
Wooden wedding rings
hand-crafted from non-tropical,
sustainable hardwoods.

Jewellery-making and other workshops

Craft workshops where you can
have fun as you make are also
great for hen parties.

www.beadshopscotland.co.uk
Workshops and repairs in Edinburgh
and East Lothian.

www.beadsunlimited.co.uk
Long-standing Brighton shop,
blog and how-tos.

www.bijouxbeads.co.uk
Beads and workshops in the
West Country.

www.cocochocolate.co.uk
Chocolate-making parties
in Edinburgh.

www.countrycupcakes.co.uk
Decorating school with award-winning
cupcake maker.

www.laughinghens.com
Knitting workshops in Cheddar.

www.themakelounge.com
Workshops and parties in London,
from cupcakes to fascinators.

www.themakeryonline.co.uk
Craft, sewing and jewellery workshops
and parties in Bath.

www.purlalpacadesigns.com
Knitting workshops in Cambridge.

www.the-beadshop.co.uk
Beading workshops in Manchester.

Groomswear

www.getethical.com
Fairtrade cufflinks.

www.junkystyling.co.uk
Fabulous menswear created
by reworking vintage pieces.

www.mossbros.co.uk
The original wedding hire company,
with everything from suits and
ties to shoes.

www.norasotamaa.com
Commissioned eco-fabric suits.

Invites

www.cherrygorgeous.co.uk
Eco-chic wedding invitations
and stationery.

www.greenleafpress.co.uk
Eco-friendly invitations and stationery.

www.hellolucky.co.uk
Gorgeous recycled and tree-free
invitations.

www.mandalayweddinginvitations.
co.uk
Recycled cards tied with post-
consumer recycled ribbons.

www.noblefineart.co.uk
Family-run letterpress printing and
hand-drawn prints.

www.park-studio.com
Designer who produces invites using eco-friendly materials.

www.seedprints.co.uk
Beautiful handmade screen-printed invitations and recycled photograph albums.

www.wrenhandmade.typepad.com
Handmade crafted invites and accessories.

Paper

www.elliepoopaper.co.uk
Ellie and Rhino Poo, plus lavender and wildflower seed.

www.greenstat.co.uk
Recycled and tree-free papers, and other stationery.

www.creativepaperwales.co.uk
Craft mill that produces Sheep Poo paper.

www.mulberrypaperandmore.com
Beautiful specialist papers, including mulberry bark.

www.tinyboxcompany.co.uk
Recycled gift boxes and ribbons made from wood derivatives.

Eco printers

www.alocalprinter.com
www.barefootpress.com
www.bigskyprint.com
www.ecofriendlyprinting.co.uk
www.ecoprintuk.com
www.kennetprint.co.uk
www.mobiusgreenprint.com

www.parklanepress.co.uk
www.seacourt.net
www.severnprint.co.uk
www.waterless.org

E-weddings

From e-vites to green web hosts:
www.ecologicalhosting.com
www.gn.apc.org
www.momentville.com
www.paperlesspost.com
www.weddingpath.co.uk

Local, organic and fairtrade food

Find your local artisan producers through the listings sites here.

www.abelandcole.co.uk
One of the original veg box providers in the UK.

www.artisancheese.co.uk
Online sales of British artisan cheeses.

www.bigbarn.co.uk
Find and buy from local food suppliers.

www.essentialtrading.co.uk
Organic and sustainable store cupboard essentials.

www.fairtrade.org.uk
The Fairtrade Foundation website, including product search.

www.finecheese.co.uk
Local cheeses and chutneys.

www.fishonline.org
Check the 'fish to eat' list for the most sustainable types to buy.

www.freerangereview.com
Enter your postcode to find local suppliers and producers.

www.lahlootea.co.uk
Specialist teas produced ethically.

www.localfoodadvisor.com
Lists farmers' markets, farm shops and recommended producers.

www.pickyourown.info
Find pick-your-own farms in the UK.

www.riverford.co.uk
The original vegetable box scheme for all your organic provisions.

www.soilassociation.org.uk
The Soil Association's website with information and stockists.

Specialist caterers

Many caterers will offer local, seasonal menus if you ask.

www.dartmoorkitchen.com
Sustainable and stylish caterers in Devon.

www.eco-cuisine.co.uk
Organic, ethical, wild and sustainable – based in London.

www.evergreencatering.co.uk
Seasonal, free-range and fairtrade catering in Bristol.

www.handmadefood.com
Organic and sustainable fine food in south-east London.

www.kateskitchenbristol.co.uk
Seasonal and local food in the West Country.

www.manicorganicsw.co.uk
Organic vegan and vegetarian
catering in the southwest.

www.mouth-music.co.uk
Contemporary vegetarian caterers
in Cambridge.

www.mrspaisleyslashings.com
Sustainable catering and event
planning from Jo Wood and the
UK's leading eco chef, Arthur Potts
Dawson. A percentage of profit
goes to a scheme to set up gardens
in schools to encourage the next
generation to grow their own.

www.organicbuffet.co.uk
Soil Association award-winning
caterer in Berkshire.

www.pieminister.co.uk
Delicious pies made with locally
sourced ingredients.

www.sfcatering.co.uk
Locally sourced, organic catering
in Yorkshire.

www.weirdigans.co.uk
Organic, solar-powered festival tent
café from West Yorkshire.

Eco-friendlier
disposable tableware

Also available from eco stores at the
end of this directory.

www.ecothefriendlyfrog.co.uk
Plates and bowls made from reed
pulp, and wooden cutlery.

www.thewholeleafco.com
Made from naturally fallen
palm leaves.

Drink

www.ashridgecider.co.uk
My favourite sparkling cider maker.

www.atlanticbrewery.co.uk
Organic beers suitable for vegans.

www.avonleighorganics.co.uk
Soil Association-certified organic
English wines.

www.englishwineweek.co.uk
English wine festival website.

www.ethicalwine.com
Online ethical wine retailer.

www.luscombe.co.uk
Delicious natural drinks, suitable
for vegans.

www.nyetimber.com
Sussex vineyard.

www.pebblebed.co.uk
Certified organic Devon wine.

www.pennardorganicwines.co.uk
Soil Association grape wine, fruit wine,
mead and cider.

www.realdrink.co.uk
Traditional cider, apple juice, cider
brandy and elderflower cordial.

www.seddlescombe
Vineyard in East Sussex and home of
the 'adopt a vine' scheme.

www.sharpham.com
Devon-made wines and cheeses.

www.vinceremos.co.uk
Organic wine specialist..

www.vintageroots.co.uk
Organic wines for every occasion.

www.westlakefarm.com
Award-winning organic apple juice
and cider.

www.wickhamvineyard.com
Award-winning English wines,
including sparkling.

www.winkleighcider.com
Established Devon cider makers –
available in bulk containers.

Cakes

www.berryscrumptious.co.uk
Scottish chocolate-dipped berries
presented as a wedding cake.

www.cakeadoodledo.co.uk
Free-range cupcakes from Devon.

www.cake-couture.com
Wholly organic cakes from Surrey.

www.cakesbyann.co.uk
Wedding cakes baked using organic
ingredients, from Larnarkshire.

www.especiallydelicious.co.uk
Gluten-free, organic, fairtrade cakes.

www.lvcc.co.uk
Little Venice Cake Company – cakes
made using organic ingredients.

www.maisiefantaisie.co.uk
Fine organic confections from London.

www.planet-cake.com
Rachel provided the cakes for the
book and bakes with eggs from her
own city garden hens in London.

www.utterlysexycafe.co.uk
Unusual, visually stunning cakes
for every wedding.

Flowers

www.tallulahrose.co.uk
The book's florist and the best
flower courses available.

www.bathorganicblooms.co.uk
Organic flowers grown with care
in Somerset.

www.bellafififlowers.co.uk
Bristol florist and ethical flower supplier.

www.countryroses.co.uk
This Suffolk provider grows roses
for all occasions.

www.catkinflowers.co.uk
Walled-garden-grown seasonal
blooms from Lincolnshire.

www.flowersbyjulieb.co.uk
Eco-friendly seasonal floristry,
based in Surrey.

www.natureslarder.net
Herb and cut flower growers in
Derbyshire, plus craft workshops.

www.realflowers.co.uk
Gorgeous British and fairtrade
cut flowers.

www.rebeccafrere.co.uk
Florist using British flowers.

www.shropshirepetals.com
Fragrant dried wheatsheaf and
lavender bouquets.

www.sweetlovingflowers.co.uk
Based in Wales, with gorgeous
sweetpeas, cornflowers and more.

www.traditionalflower.co.uk
English-grown cut flowers and herbs.

Decorations

www.aztecarts.co.uk
Recycled aluminium bowls with bright
enameled interiors.

www.corsetlacedmannequins.co.uk
Vintage mannequins, picnic hampers
and crockery.

www.coralquay.co.uk
Home of beautiful fairtrade
decorations, trinkets and accessories.

www.devondriftwooddesigns.co.uk
Gorgeous natural decorations,
including beautiful driftwood trees.

www.ecobunting.co.uk
Beautiful bunting made from
waste materials.

www.fairwindonline.com
From hand-painted picnicware to
hanging glass tea-light holders.

www.skylantern.co.uk
Beautiful biodegradable
paper sky lanterns.

www.tatteredandtorn.co.uk
Beautiful hand-dyed bunting made
from vintage materials.

www.therecyclewarehouse.com
From recycled lanterns to
seed-paper cards.

www.zigzagbunting.co.uk
Eco-friendly cotton bunting.

Furniture, crockery and decoration hire

www.amostcuriousparty.co.uk
London vintage china hire.

www.ecomoon.co.uk
I can hire out china, props, vintage bits
and pieces for weddings.

www.jongor4hire.com
Furniture hire in Bristol and Portsmouth.

www.pebble-in-the-pond.co.uk
Vintage crockery and organic linens,
near Manchester.

www.prestigecateringhire.co.uk
Everything from trestle tables to cutlery
in southwest England.

www.vintageevent.co.uk
China and props for a vintage
celebration in the north of England.

Soy and beeswax candles

www.alotofcandles.co.uk
Organic plant-wax candles.

www.blossomcandles.com
Handmade poured pillar and floating
beeswax candles.

www.brighterblessings.co.uk
Hand-rolled beeswax candles.

www.fallingstar.co.uk
Handmade, ethical soy candles.

www.hapibean.co.uk
The best handmade soy tea lights
in the UK.

www.jonathanwardlondon.com
Delicious hand-poured organic
scented candles.

Favours

www.tree2mydoor.com
Native tree gifts in eco-friendly packaging.

Ethical chocolate favour gifts are available from:
www.blakesorganicchocolate.ie
www.boojabooja.com
www.chocaid.com
www.chocolala.co.uk
www.divinechocolate.com
www.duchyoriginals.com
www.hotelchocolat.co.uk
www.malagasy.co.uk
www.montezumas.co.uk
www.traidcraftshop.co.uk
www.venturefoods.com

Natural beauty

www.alexandrasoveral.co.uk
Bespoke natural perfumes, bath oils and skincare.

www.barefoot-botanicals.com
Try their rose-scented body sculpt body cream for defined curves.

www.comvitahuni.com
Delicious Huni skincare, which uses manuka honey.

www.drhauschka.co.uk
Established natural skincare brand.

www.elysambre.co.uk
Fabulous colourful make-up for all skins.

www.florame.co.uk
Organic natural perfume range.

www.florascent.co.uk
Natural fragrances produced by traditional methods.

www.great-elm.com
Lovely organic, plant-based, restorative skincare.

www.jowoodorganics.co.uk
Gorgeous perfumes for organic girls.

www.jurlique.com
Australian beauty products, with the best body scrub.

www.lavera.co.uk
Fabulous affordable natural make-up and skincare; Touch of Sun is a beauty bag must.

www.lavere.co.uk
Ethical skincare designed for thirtysomethings-plus.

www.livingnature.com
Pure skincare from New Zealand.

www.logona.co.uk
Make-up and skincare – and the iconic wrinkle therapy cream.

www.madara.co.uk
Natural skincare to suit all skin types.

www.naturisimo.com
The home of Luzern luxury natural skincare.

www.nealsyardremedies.co.uk
The largest collection of organic skincare in the UK.

www.nudeskincare.co.uk
The best natural make-up remover; try their night oil for perfect skin, too.

www.purist.com
Gorgeous bath and body products for bride and groom from A'kin.

www.spieziaorganics.com
Cornish organic and natural skincare.

www.theorganicpharmacy.com
Home of organic skincare and make-up.

www.weleda.co.uk
Established super-ethical skincare brand.

My favourite online beauty stores

www.beautybazaar.co.uk
www.lovelula.com
www.naturisimo.co.uk
www.theremustbeabetterway.co.uk

The big day

www.ecochariots.com
Pedal-powered pedicabs, based in London.

www.ecomoon.co.uk
Organises eco-friendly weddings and events to suit all budgets.

www.herefordpedicabs.com
Zero-emission pedicabs.

www.onyabags.co.uk
Buy one to hold your wedding day kit, and to use after the day.

www.orglamic.co.uk
Professional make-up artist using natural cosmetics.

www.thebiglemon.co.uk
Ethical, eco-friendly buses for hire running on recycled cooking oil.

www.unionphotography.co.uk
Marc was our photographer for this book and also covers weddings and events.

Petal confetti

www.jerseylavender.co.uk
Bags of fragrant lavender heads.

www.petalpot.co.uk
Biodegradable petal confetti.

www.realflowers.co.uk
Fresh rose petal confetti.

www.shropshirepetals.com
British-grown natural petal confetti.

Wedding lists

www.ecocentric.co.uk
Ethical and eco-friendly wares.

www.fairtradegiftlist.co.uk
Fairtrade gifts for all.

http://giveincelebration.
cancerresearchuk.org
Cancer Research website for
gift donations and favours.

www.henandhammock.co.uk
Gorgeous ethical outdoor living and
garden wares.

www.justgiving.co.uk
Charity donation website.

www.nigelsecostore.com
Brilliant online eco store.

www.oxfamunwrapped.co.uk
Many alternative gifts that benefit
less developed countries.

www.rainforestconcern.org
Sponsor an acre of rainforest.

www.thealternativeweddinglist.co.uk
Gift list benefiting many charities.

www.thegreenshop.co.uk
Sustainable gifts for all.

www.thegreenweddinglist.co.uk
Unique and varied charity gift lists.

www.thevintageweddinglist.co.uk
From classic vintage books to
sculpted glass jugs.

Honeymoons and eco hotels

Also see the hotels and guides
in the Venues section.

www.argyllhoteliona.co.uk
Local and organic produce on
a tiny Scottish island.

www.canopyandstars.co.uk
Cool camping, in yurts to tree houses,
from Alastair Sawday.

www.climatecare.org
Credible carbon offset company.

www.ecofriendlyhotels.co.uk
Eco-friendly hotels all over the world.

www.ecoescape.org
Sustainable and eco-friendly
holidays in the United Kingdom
and Ireland.

www.greentraveller.co.uk
This website is all you need to
plan your green break.

www.naturalretreats.com
Eco-friendly self-catering holiday lets
in the UK and Ireland.

www.organicholidays.co.uk
Fabulous organic hotels, farm
and self-catering accommodation
across the world.

www.responsibletravel.co.uk
The world's leading travel agent for
responsible holidays.

www.seat61.com
How to travel the world by train
and ship.

www.underthethatch.co.uk
Stylish, quirky and ethically responsible
holiday cottages.

www.uplandescapes.com
Eco-friendly walking holidays.

www.yurtworks.co.uk
Yurt holidays in Cornwall.

Online eco and fairtrade stores and listings

www.allthingseco.co.uk
www.ecotopia.co.uk
www.ecocentric.co.uk
www.ethicaljunction.org
www.ethicalsuperstore.co.uk
www.ethicalweddings.com
www.livingethically.co.uk
www.naturalcollection.co.uk
www.nigelsecostore.co.uk
www.thefairtradestore.co.uk

Glossary

BDIH
The European organisation that certifies beauty products as being natural (www.kontrollierte-naturkosmetik.de).

Biomass boiler
A boiler powered by wood chips or pellets that can be used to heat water or as part of a central heating system.

Carbomers
Synthetic polymers, or plastic-like substances, used to thicken cosmetics and stop them from separating.

DEAs
Compounds of diethanolamine, which have a range of uses in cosmetics and skincare products. Also look for TEA, or triethanolamine. There are concerns that these can react with certain other ingredients to form cancer-causing chemicals, which have led to restrictions on how they can be used.

DBP
A type of phthalate.

Ecocert
French organic and sustainability certification body for food, cosmetics and textiles (www.ecocert.com).

Embodied energy
The total energy required to make a product, from extraction and manufacture to transport. Some analyses also include the energy required to disassemble and dispose of the product after use.

GMOs
Genetically modified organisms.

Mineral oil
Also listed as paraffinum liquidum. Clear, odourless oil derived from petroleum. Believed to interfere with the body's own protective oily barrier.

OFC
Organic Food Chain, an Australian certification body (www.organicfoodchain.com.au).

Parabens
Widely used as artificial preservatives in cosmetics. There is concern that some may be carcinogenic.

Phthalates
Used as softeners in plastics, but found widely in products such as hairspray and perfumes.

SLS
Sodium lauryl sulphate is a harsh and potentially skin irritating detergent used as a foaming agent in shampoos and toothpaste. Some natural products use sodium laureth sulphate as an alternative, but there are questions about this compound, too.

Sulphates
A catch-all term employed to mean detergents such as sodium lauryl and laureth sulphate and other similar compounds. Not all chemicals listed on labels as a sulphate are detergents.

USDA
The US Department of Agriculture, which oversees and sets the regulations for organic certification in the USA (www.usda.gov).

Note:
The use of all chemicals in cosmetics is under constant review and regulation by organisations such as the European Commission (ec.europa.eu), the US Food and Drug Administration (www.fda.gov) and NICNAS in Australia (www.nicnas.gov.au).

Seasonal Fruit and Vegetables

Note that January includes some produce that comes into season late in the year but continues through winter.

January

Vegetables
Cabbages
Cauliflower
Cavolo nero
Jerusalem artichokes
Kale
Purple sprouting broccoli

Fruit
Champagne rhubarbLate
pears, such as Conference
Seville oranges for
marmalade and other citrus
fruits (imported)

February

Vegetables
Greenhouse lettuces

March

Vegetables
Chives
Nettles
Watercress

April

Vegetables
Early baby salad leaves and
winter lettuce
Radishes
Sorrel
Spinach
Wild garlic

May

Vegetables
Asparagus
New potatoes
New season carrots
Wild rocket

June

Vegetables
Autumn-planted onions
Broad beans
Lettuces
Peas and mangetout
Tomatoes from greenhouses

Fruit (and flowers)
Cherries
Elderflowers
Gooseberries
Redcurrants
Strawberries

July

Vegetables
Artichokes
Beetroot
Cauliflowers
Chanterelle mushrooms
Courgettes
French and runner beans
Garlic
Onions
Tomatoes grown outdoors

Fruit
Blackcurrants
Blueberries
Raspberries

August

Vegetables
Aubergines
Broccoli
Cep mushrooms (porcini)
Chard
Cucumber
Fennel
Oyster mushrooms
Sweetcorn

Fruit
Apples (early varieties)
Apricots
Autumn raspberries
Blackberries
Damsons
Plums

September

Vegetables
Borlotti beans and other
pulses for drying
Cabbages
Chillis
Kale
Peppers
Squashes and pumpkins

Fruit
Apples
Elderberries
Greengages
Pears

Nuts
Hazelnuts

October

Vegetables
Celeriac

Fruit
Apples for storing
over winter
Crab apples
Grapes
Quinces
Sloes

Nuts
Walnuts

November

Vegetables
Brussels sprout tops
Cavolo nero
Chicory and radicchio
Jerusalem artichokes
Parsnips
Swedes

Nuts
Chestnuts

December

Vegetables
Brussels sprouts
Spring greens

Fruit
Champagne rhubarb
(forced)
Citrus fruits (imported)

Seasonal Flowers

January

Dogwood stems
Hellebores
Hyacinths grown indoors
Snowdrops
Winter cherry blossom
Witch hazel stems in flower

February

Camellias
Dwarf irises
Narcissi (early)
Ornamental quince blossom

March

Catkins and willow
branches
Cherry blossom
Daffodils
Forsythia
Hyacinths
Tulips
Wood anemones

April

Forget-me-nots
Fritillaries
Lily-of-the-valley
Magnolia
Plum and apple blossom
Violets in pots and
for edible blossoms

May

Alliums
Bluebells
Bupleurums
Calendula
Calla lilies
Campanulas
Cornflowers
Cow parsley and
other umbellifers
Foxgloves
Irises
Lady's mantle
Lilac
Oriental poppies
Peonies
Roses
Snapdragons
Stocks
Sweet peas

June

Astrantias
Lavender
Monardas
Nigella
Sweet williams

July

Bells of Ireland
Cosmos
Delphiniums
Hydrangeas
Lilies
Phlox
Scabious
Zinnias

August

Echinaceas
Fresh hops
Grasses
Love-lies-bleeding
Sunflowers

September

Agapanthus
Asters
Dahlias
Eryngiums
Japanese anemones
Sedums

October

Hips and crab apples
Maples and other
autumn foliage
Nerines

November

Chrysanthemums
Pansies
Winter-flowering
honeysuckle stems

December

Amaryllis grown indoors
Cyclamen in pots
Holly
Ivy
Paperwhite narcissi
grown indoors
Viburnum blossom stems

If you do buy imported
flowers, look for the following
accreditations to make
sure they are grown in a
socially and environmentally
responsible way:

EcoBlooms
Veriflora
Fairtrade
Transitional
Florverde
Ecocert
Rainforest Alliance
Fair Labor Practices
FlorEcuador

Index

Page numbers in **bold** refer to illustrations.

A

accessories 75-89
  bags 86, **87**, 88, **89**, 170
  beads 24, **25**, 70, 80-81, **80**
  boleros 82
  camisoles **84**, 85
  corsages 67, **67**, 77, 81, 82, 83, **83**, 189
    fabric flower 68, **69**
    fixing 145
  rings **78**, 79
  underwear 85
  (see also: jewellery)
air conditioning 38
albums 30
allergies 151, 175
almonds, sugared 170
aloe vera gel 182, 192
animal testing 176
antique weddings 23
  jewellery 76, 81
  postcards 101
  wooden printing stamps 96, **97**, 98
arboretums 47
aromatherapy oils 178, 179
artists, commissioning 20
assistance
  from family and friends 26, 28, 56, 112, 124, 143
    baking 127
    dresses 62
  on-the-day 186, 191

B

Bach Rescue Remedy 178, 186
bags 86, **87**
  bridesmaid tote 188, **189**
  hessian 156
  lavender 170
  Onya 193
  wedding day 88, **89**
bamboo 64, 85
banana paper 93

barbecues 116
barns 44
beach weddings **34**, 47, 156, 183
beads 70, 80-81, **80**
beauty preparations 173-185
  bath soak 179
  for blemishes 176
  body scrub 179
  face masks 178
    edible 180-181
  finishing touches 182
  hair 182-183, **183**
  make-up 176-177
  miracle creams 177
  nails 182
  organic skincare 174-175, 192
  perfume 182
  for puffy eyes 176
  spa treatments 178
  stress-relieving 178-179
  teeth 182
bed and breakfast, organic 41, 192
Bedouin tents 42
beeswax 164
  candles 168
  in makeup 175, 176
berries, as decoration 20, 132
bicycles 159
biodynamic flowers 140
biodynamic food 110
biscuits, heart 170, **170**
boleros 82
botanical gardens 47
bouquets 144, **144**, 145, **145**, 162
  hand-tied 146, **147**
bows, sugar paste 134
boxes, for favours **95**, 170
bridal shops 61
bridesmaids
  clothing 58, 73, 83
  flowers 144
  tote bag 188, **189**
  wedding day bag 88, **89**
British Trust for Conservation 192
budgets 28, 35, 54, 167, 192
bunting 48, **154**, 160, 167

buttonholes 144, 145
buttons 80
  vintage 68, 101, 160

C

cakes 120-137
  alternative 131
  baking 122, 124-125
  cheese 131
  choosing 122
  decorating 132-135
  displaying **120**, 123, **123**, 125, **125**, **129**, 136, **137**
  as favours 136
  icing 123, **125**, 127, **129**, 131, 133
  individual 131
  ingredients 122
  mousse 131
  professional bakers 122
  tiered/stacked **120**, 122, **123**, 125, **132**, **133**
  transporting 124
  (see also: cupcakes)
calligraphy 98
camisoles **84**, 85
campfires 116
camping, for guests 42
candelabras 168
candles 48, 168
  teacup **27**, 164, **165**
car-boot sales 56, 76, 86
carbon footprint 18, 39, 192
  albums 30
  cakes 122
  chocolate 131
  dresses 61, 65
  flowers 82, 140
  food 20, 108
  paper 92, 103
  travel 35, 41
carbon neutrality 23, 43
card holders **102**, 103
castles 44
caterers, choosing 108, 111
catering
  DIY 112, **113**, 114-115, 124-125
  outdoor 116-117

cellophane 136
ceremonies 30, 35
  civil 41, 44
charity shops 23, 86, 191
  crockery 112, 160
  dresses 58, **58**, 59, **59**
  jewellery 76
cheeses, as cake 131
chemicals, avoiding 18
  dry-cleaning 66
  jewellery 79
  in nail varnish 182
  pesticides 61
  in photographs 30
  skincare 174, 175, 176
  venue decor 38
chocolate 24, 127, 131
  curls 135
  fairtrade 24, 131
chokers 82, 83
churches 44
chutney 114, **114**, **115**
cider 119
clothing 70, **71**, 82, **83**, **84**, 85
  for bridesmaids 58, 73, 85
  for grooms 73, 75
  for page boys 58, 73
  (see also: dresses)
cocktails, organic 119
collage 98, 101
colour schemes 24, 48, 73, 85
  cake 122
  dresses 54
  dyes 64, 73
  invitations 96
confetti, biodegradable 152, **153**
containers 148-149, 151, 167
contemporary weddings
  cake design 125, 127
  flowers 148
coordinated look 26, 73
  cake 122
  flowers 20
    bouquets 144
  hair 182
  stationery 93
cordials , homemade 119

corsages 67, **67**, 77, 81, 82, 83, **83**
  fabric flower 68, **69**
  fixing 145
  for tote bag 189
corsets 85
cotton, organic 64, 66, 85
country house parties 44
crockery 112, 160
Cruck marquees 39, 42, **43**
cupcakes 126-129, **126-129**
  displaying 127, 136, **137**
  Lou's gluten-free lemon 128-129, **128-129**

D

daisy chains 81, **81**
dance floors 43
decorations 154-171
  berries 20, 132
  bunting 48, **154**, 160, 167
  for cake display 136
  for cakes 132-135
  for chairs 50, **51**
  cheap 167
  edible 134-135
  fairtrade 167
  handmade 162, **163**
  hiring 167
  natural 156, **157**
  original/unusual **158**, 159
  seasonal 156, **157**
  seed paper butterflies 95
delegation 186, 191
Demeter 110, 140
designer
  samples 58
  stationery 97
Diamond Council 79
diamonds, ethical 79
dietary sensitivities 119, 176
DIY weddings 26
  catering 112, **113**, 114-115, 124-125
  invitations 98-101
dresses **25**, 53-73
  alterations 67
  antique 56
  borrowed 66
  cleaning 66
  covering marks 66
  ethical 58
  fairtrade 61
  and flowers 54
  free 66-67

handmade/homemade 62-63, **183**
  hiring 66
  new **60**, 61
  online purchases 56
  retro 56, 57, **57**
  second-hand 56, 58, **58**, 59, **59**
  sewing tips 62
  storage 66
  style 54-55, 56, **56**, 57, **57**
    and body shape 55
    and bouquets 144
  trains 70
  transporting 35
  vintage 56, **56**, 57, **57**, **58**
    fabrics 65
    patterns 62
dressmakers 24, 26
  working with 62-63
driftwood 24, 136, 156
drink 119
  teas 117
dry-cleaning 66
dyes, natural vegetable 64, 101

E

e-vites 24, 103
eco honeymoons 104
eco awareness 18
eco-chic weddings 24
eco hotels 24, 35, 41, 192
eco photography 30
eco stationery 97
embellishments 65
  for bags 86
  beads 70
  for bicycles 159
  bouquets 144
  for guest book 104
  for invitations 98-99
  posting 98
  ribbons 67, 70
  for shoes 70.**71**
energy
  generation 38, 41
  renewable 38, 41, 103, 176
  saving 44
envelopes, recycled/homemade 93
environmental impact 18, 26, 79
equipment hire 48
escort cards **102**, 103
essential oils 175, 178, 179, 192
ethical issues 18, 44

gifts 104
rings 79
shopping 61
(see also: fairtrade)
eye masks, lavender 181

F

fabrics 48
  eco-friendly/natural 64-65, 73
  fairtrade 61, 64
  natural 20, 62, 85
  reclaimed 101
  remnants 65
  washing 85
face masks 175, 178
  edible 180-181
fairs, wedding 61
fairtrade 18, 38
  card holders **102**, 103
  chocolate 24, 131
  decorations 167
  dresses 61
  fabrics 61, 64
  flowers 24, 140
  food 110
  gifts 104
  jewellery 79
  papers 92
  underwear 85
Fairtrade Foundation 110
family and friends
  help from 26, 28, 56, 112, 124, 143
    baking 127
    on the day 186, 191
    dresses 62
famous 20th-century weddings 23
farmers' markets 108, 143
favours
  boxes for **95**, 170
  chutney **115**
  homemade 156, 170
  jewellery 160, **161**
  seeds 170
  soaps 24, 162
  tree and herb 156
festivals 192
floristry workshops 140
florists, professional 140, 145
flower girls 58, 73
flower waters 182
flowers 138-153
  as accessories 82

biodynamic 140
for bridesmaids 144
buttonholes 144
as cake decoration 132, **133**
containers for 148-149, 151, 167
for coordinated look 20
displays 148-149, 151
and dresses 54
dried 143
edible 110
fabric 162
fairtrade 24, 140
foliage 151
giving away 152
growing 143
organic 140
paper 132, 162, **163**
petal confetti 152, **153**
recycling 152, 191
seasonal 139, 140, 143, 156
  calendar 217
silk 132
sourcing 46, 143
stress remedies 178
wild 143
(see also: bouquets)
foliage 151
follies 44, 47
food
  biodynamic 110
  caterers 108, 111
  fairtrade 110
  foraging 20, 111
  gluten-free 128
  homemade 112, **113**, 114-115
    heart biscuits 170, **171**
    sugared almonds 170
    truffles 170
  local 20, 38
  organic 38, 110
  seasonal 20, 108, 112
    calendar 216
  shared preparation 26
  slow 111
  tartlets 131
  tea parties 117
  transporting 117
  (see also: cakes; menus)
food miles 20, 26
foraging 20, 111
foreign weddings 35
Forest Stewardship Council 92
Freecycle 66, 167
furniture hire 23, 42, 48

G

Garden Organic 143
garden parties 23
gardens
  botanical 47
  cottage 143
  wildflower 41
garters 85
gay and lesbian weddings 30
gift lists 24, 104
gifts, ethical 104
glass
  bottles 167
  ornaments 162
  sea 80
glitter, edible 134
gloves 85
gluten-free recipes 128
gold 79
gowns (see: dresses)
green venues 18, 38-39, 41
GreenEarth process 66
grooms, clothing 73
guest books 104
guests
  camping for 42
  help with catering 112, 124, 127
  numbers of 39

H

hair 182, 183, **183**
hair-bands 81, 182
hampers 116, **116**
hand masks, tomato
and yogurt 181
hand-fastings 30, 39, 41
handmade weddings 26
  bags 86
  dresses 62-63, **183**
  invitations 98-101
  papers 92-93
  signs 159
  (see also homemade projects)
hay bales 148
Hedgerow Sling (recipe) 119
heirlooms 76
hemp 64, 66
hemp silk 24, 64, 66, 82, **84**, 85
hen parties 35
herbs 112, 151
  as bath soak 179
  as buttonholes 144
  as favours 156

hiring
  decorations 167
  dresses 66
  equipment 48, 112, 124, 191
  furniture 23, 42, 48
  suits 73
  tents 42
historic buildings 44
hog roasts 117
homemade projects
  bridesmaid tote bag 188, **189**
  chair decoration 50, **51**
  chocolate curls 135
  edible sugared petals 135
  fabric flower corsage 68, **69**
  hand-tied wedding bouquet
  146, **147**
  hessian bag for favours 156
  Lou's gluten-free lemon
cupcakes 128-129, **128-129**
  Lou's homemade chutney 114,
114, 115
  sugar paste bows 134
  teacup candles 164, **165**
  wedding day bag 88, **89**
  wildflower seed paper 94-95,
94, 95
  (see also: handmade
weddings)
honeymoons 104, 191, 192, 193
hotels
  eco 24, 35, 41
  organic 41
humanist weddings 30
humour, sense of 186

I

icing 123, **125**, 127, **129**, 131, 133
inks, vegetable-based 30, 96
invitations 91-105
  e-vites 24, 103
  embellishments 98-99
  handmade 98-101
  paper types 92-93, **93**
  printing 96-97, **96, 97**
ivy 151

J

jam jars
  for flower display 149, 167
  lanterns 159, 168
jewellery 76, **76**, 77, **77**
  beads 24, **25**, 70, 80-81, **80**

cleaning 79
favours 160, **161**
rings, ethical **78**, 79
vintage 76, 132
workshops 79

K

kata tents 42, 191
Kimberley Process 79

L

lace 86, **87**, 144, **144**, 159, 162
lanterns 159, 168
lavender 50
  bags 170
  chair decoration 50, **51**
  eye masks 181
leaves 104, 156
  printing with 98
legalities 30, 35, 41
lemonade, homemade 119
letterpress printing 96, 97
licences
  civil ceremonies 41
  liquor 42
  marquee 42, 48
lighting 48, 159, 168, **169**
linen 64, 73
lino cuts 99, 101
liqueurs 119
lists 28
local
  food 20, 38
  parks 47
  venues 48

M

make-up 176-177
map paper 92
Marine Stewardship Council 110
markets 76
  farmers' 108, 143
marquees 42
  Cruck 39, 42, **43**
  licences 48
marrying abroad 35
mementoes 191
menus 107-119
  seasonal 108
  (see also: food)
meringues, mini 131
mills 44

mineral water 119
mirrors 159
mulled wine and cider 119
music 23, 35, 42

N

nails 182
name tags 97
  as favours 170
  pebbles 24, 156
  recycled 26
  seed paper 95
  wooden 162
Natural Wedding Planner 202
natural weddings 18
  cupcakes 127
  fabrics 20, 62, 85
nettles 64
notebook **32-33**, 54, 62, 122

O

online purchases
  dresses 56
  Freecycle 66, 167
organic
  bed and breakfast 41, 192
  cocktails 119
  cotton 64, 66, 85
  flowers 140
  food 38, 110
  hotels 41
  products 38, 41
  skincare **174**, 175, 178, 179,
  180-181, 192
ornaments 160
  glass 162
outdoor weddings 30, **46**, 47,
117, 122, 156
Oxfam Bridal 58, **58**, **59**

P

packaging
  recycled 176
  reducing 26
packing 35
  for honeymoon 193
page boys 58, 73
paper flowers 132, 162, **163**
paper scrolls 170
paper types, alternative 92-93
paperless weddings 103
parks 47

pastillage 133

peace silk 24, 61, 64, 66, 82, 85

pearls 81

pebbles, as name tags 24, 156

perfumes 182

perry 119

pesticides, avoiding 61

petals

   confetti 152, **153**

   in paper 93

photography, eco-friendly 30

place names

   retro/vintage 161

   (see also: name tags)

planning

   Natural Wedding Planner 202

   notebook **32-33**, 54, 62, 122

platinum 79

pots 151, 167

presents (see: gift lists; gifts)

printing

   by hand 98-99

   letterpress 96, 97

   styles of 96-97

   waterless 96-97

priority lists 28

R

raffia 26, 99, 101, 132, 151, 167

Raven, Sarah 143

recycling 191

   beads 80

   envelopes 93

   flowers 152, 191

   gold/platinum 79

   paper 92

   plastic for ribbons 96

   printer cartridges 97

retro weddings, ideas 23, 160, 161

ribbons 67, 70, 81, 85, 101, 132, 145

   chair decoration 50, **51**

   as choker 82, 83

   recycled 96, **96**

   in trees 159

rings, ethical **78**, 79

S

scarves 82

screen-printing 98, 99

sculptures, recycled 162

Seasonal Flower Calendar 217

Seasonal Fruit and Vegetable Calendar 216

seasonal weddings 20

   decorations 156, **157**

   drink 117, 119

   flowers 139, 140, 143, 156

   food 20, 108, 122

second-hand, dresses 56, 58, **58**, 59, **59**

seed paper 93

   wildflower 94-95

seeds

   as favours 170

   in paper 94, **95**

sewing tips 62

shells 101

shoes 70, **71**

signs, handmade 159

silk, hemp 24, 64, 66, 82, **84**, 85

silk, peace 24, 61, 64, 66, 82, 85

skin, sensitive 64, 66, 175

skincare, organic **174**, 175, 178, 179, 180-181, 192

sky lanterns 159

slow food 111

slow travel 192

soap-making workshops 162

soaps 48

   as favours 24, 162

spas 178, 192

stag parties 35

stamps, for printing **97**, 98, 101, 159

stationery

   designer eco 97

   escort cards **102**, 103

   guest books 104

   thank-you cards 103

   vintage 101

   (see also: invitations)

stress, avoiding 178-179, 182, 186

style 17-35

   dresses 54-55, 56, **56**, 57, **57**

   eco-chic 24

   handmade 26

   natural 18

   seasonal 20

   vintage 23

sugar paste 134

swishing parties 66

T

table numbers **157**

table plans 162

tablecloths 23, 48

tags

   name 24, 26

   for wishes 95, 104, **105**

tans, fake 182

tartlets 131

tea lights 132, 151, 168

tea parties 117

teacup candles **27**, 164, **165**

teas, speciality 117, **117**

teeth 182

tents **39**, 42, **43**

thank-you cards 103

themes, seasonal 20

tiaras, beaded 80, **80**

tipis **39**, 42, 191, 192

topiary, hired 24

trains (of dresses) 70

transport 24

   sustainable 192

tree-free papers 92

trees, as favours 156

truffles 170

U

umbrellas, golfing 186

underwear 85

V

veils 70

venues 37-51

   green 18, 38-39, 41

   historic buildings 44

   local 48

   outdoors 30, **46**, 47, 117, 122

   tents 42

   transforming 48, **49**, 50, **51**

   and vision 39

village halls 48

vintage weddings 23

   buttons 68, 101, 160

   candlesticks 168

   crockery 112, 160

   cupcakes 127

   dresses 56, **56**, 57, **57**, 58

      fabrics 65

      patterns 62

   jewellery 76, 132

   stationery 101

   themed decorations 160, 161

volunteering holidays 192

W

waste management strategies 38

waterless printing 96-97

weather, inclement 186

websites 103

wedding day

   enjoying 186

   kit 186

   websites 103

wedding fairs 61

wellington boots 70, 149, 186

wheatsheaves 143

wildflower gardens 41

wildflower seed paper 94, **95**

wildflowers 143

wildlife conservation centres 47

wine, organic **118**, 119

wire 101

wishes trees 104, **105**

wood cuts 99

woodblock printing 96, **97**, 98

workshops 98, 99

   floristry 140

   jewellery 79

   soap-making 162

wraps 82, **83**

Y

yurts 42, 191, 192

Acknowledgements

I would like to express my thanks to everyone who has been involved in this book, right from the start, my sincere appreciation goes out to them all.

Firstly, to my gorgeous friends who agreed to model for us: Lauren Bunclark, Emma Savage, Karen Matthews, Esther Lincoln, Sophie Shenstone, Vicky Millar, Maya Gavin, Jo Illsley and Rachel Wardley, along with newlyweds Lisa and Pedro and Tom and Clare, flower girls Sadie and Angelica, and the garden party wedding guests. You were all stars, even in the rain.

Secondly, to our professional team of wedding specialists who all so kindly gave their time: Karen and Lee Matthews from Lee Matthews Hair Studio Ltd, Rachel Hill from Planet Cake, Joanna Sinska from Josi, and Rachel Wardley from Tallulah Rose Flowers.

Thirdly, a huge thank you to my best friend, Justyn Turnbull, who let us invade his house, lent us numerous props from his collection and cooked us the most delicious food, which can be seen in the Menu chapter.

A big, big, thank you also goes to Caroline Harris, my editor and friend, who has held my hand and guided me through this whole process with patience, sound advice and many cups of peppermint tea. I would also like to thank Marc Wilson for taking such beautiful photographs, Shelley Doyle for her inspired designs, and editorial assistant Harriet Steeds, who helped enormously.

Finally I would like to thank my fiancé, Zac. This book really would not have been possible without his constant support, love, serenity and belief in me and my idea.

Many people and companies have also donated their time or products, or allowed us to use their space for the photo shoots. Special thanks go to Jessica Charleston, Jo Illsley at Bath Organic Blooms, Sue Harper at Sweet Loving Flowers, Kate Smith at The Makery, Marylyn and Philip at Rocks East Woodland, Kate Robinson, Janet Meadowcroft and Jill Martin for use of their lovely homes, Adam and Claire Scott-Bardwell, Jessica and Ben Eyers, Louise McGraw, Prestige Catering Hire, Duncan at The Thoughtful Bread Company, Di Francis of Avonleigh Organic Vineyard, Debbie Coutts from Tattered and Torn, Danaë Duthy of Country Roses, Oxfam Bridal, Nikki from Country Cupcakes, Wendy Morray-Jones, Shropshire Petals, Bramley and Gage, Great Western Wine, Neal's Yard Remedies, Great Elm Physick Garden, Lavera, Logona, Sante, Elysambre, Peachy Keen Organics, Trevarno, Jonathan Ward, Jo Wood Organics, Mandara, Living Nature, Luzern, A'kin, Nude, Jurlique, Organic Blue, Organic Pharmacy, REN, Butter London, Kimia and Barefoot Botanicals.

Additional photography: page 25 (sea-glass beads, heart pebbles, beach track) and page 98, Caroline Harris; page 34, © iofoto/Fotolia.com; page 39 and page 202, PapaKåta; page 41 and page 46, Sheepdrove Organic Farm; page 43, Cruck Marquees; page 47, © Marcus Kleppe/Fotolia.com; page 75, family photographs, with thanks to Jackie Carr, Joan and Austen, and Joy and Barry; page 193, © MN Studio/Fotolia.com; page 194, Ruth Brown; page 200 © Marc Wilson/Getty Images.